CONFESSIONS

of an EVENT
PLANNER

CONFESSIONS

of an EVENT
PLANNER

**Case Studies from the Real World of
Events—How to Handle the Unexpected
and How to Be a Master of Discretion**

Judy Allen

John Wiley & Sons Canada, Ltd.

Library and Archives Canada Cataloguing in Publication Data

Allen, Judy, 1952–
 Confessions of an event planner : case studies from the real world of events : how to handle the unexpected and how to be a master of discretion / Judy Allen.

ISBN 978-0-470-16018-3

 1. Special events—Planning. 2. Special events industry. I. Title.

GT3405.A452 2009   394.2'068   C2008-907817-9

Production Credits
Cover and Interior Design: Adrian So
Cover Photo: Arian So
Typesetter: Thomson Digital
Printer: Friesens

ENVIRONMENTAL BENEFITS STATEMENT

John Wiley saved the following resources by printing the pages of this book on chlorine free paper made with 100% post-consumer waste.

TREES	WATER	ENERGY	SOLID WASTE	GREENHOUSE GASES
35	12,618	24	1,620	3,040
FULLY GROWN	GALLONS	MILLION BTUs	POUNDS	POUNDS

Calculations based on research by Environmental Defense and the Paper Task Force.
Manufactured at Friesens Corporation

Editorial Credits
Executive Editor: Karen Milner
Project Coordinator: Pauline Ricablanca

John Wiley & Sons Canada, Ltd.
6045 Freemont Blvd.
Mississauga, Ontario
L5R 4J3

Printed in Canada

1 2 3 4 5 FP 13 12 11 10 09

This book is dedicated with love to Joe Thomas Shane, whom I am honored to call my 2jproductions business partner and so much more. You mean the world to me. Thank you for all the knowledge you have brought into my life personally and professionally. There is no one I could imagine sharing the exciting, new life journey in front of us other than you. Coming together with you has opened up a whole world of possibilities that fills me and fuels me with a new sense of purpose, passion and play and has brought clarity, direction, consciousness and inner knowing as to what is meant to come next. You challenge my mind, my creativity and my way of being in a way no one else ever has and I thank you for the incredible life-changing gifts that knowing you has given me. I believe that everything in life happens for a divine reason and I am looking forward to discovering all that we are meant to create and do together and through our company, 2jproductions, and bring to each other and the world.

CONTENTS

PREFACE

Confessions of an Event Planner: Case Studies from the Real World of Events—How to Handle the Unexpected and How to Be a Master of Discretion is a collection of fictionalized case studies that follows one corporate event planning company around the world. It showcases real-life scenarios both novice and experienced event planners can encounter on the job during actual event execution. Woven throughout the book are learning lessons and business ethical and etiquette situations based on actual occurrences in the industry that are played out time and time again around the world. They are meant to open the door for discussion and problem-solving exercises both in university and college classrooms around the world and in event planning and corporate business offices, with staff working together with their company's lawyers and financial controllers to determine what should be done in specific situations and to establish and define company policies, procedures and protocol in the office and on-site. This in turn helps to protect the individual, the event planning company, their event suppliers and event venues, the corporate client and their guests from legal ramifications. Not knowing what to do when an event planning crisis occurs or what steps to take to prevent one from happening can be costly both personally and professionally to those involved and to the corporations hosting and orchestrating the event.

Confessions of an Event Planner is a case study workbook/office training manual that offers students and new and established industry employees a behind-the-scenes look into the perceived glamorous world of business entertaining—from boardrooms to re-sort guest bedrooms—by a fictional event planning company owner as she travels the globe creating one-of-a-kind corporate, social and celebrity events for her clients. The intention of this book is to make sure that event planners, their clients and suppliers are well pre-pared going on-site, where being ready to handle the sorts of real-life scenarios described here is essential. Event planners must know the appropriate course of action that they need to take to protect them-selves, their company, their client, their guests and their suppliers if guests (or staff or suppliers) go wild during their event. Also, clients and suppliers need to know the course of action their individual company lawyers and advisors want them to take as well.

These special events are fuelled by corporate budgets that range from modest to those that exceed millions of dollars to en-tertain, educate or enlighten their attendees. Events can range from one-day local meetings to events that include first-class air travel, private jets, stays in six- and seven-star resorts in luxury suites and major pampering—no matter the budget, the venue or the event style—with participants being wooed, wined and dined to show client appreciation, introduce guests to new products at company product launches, bring employees together for an out-of-town conference, or reward top sales staff at an over-the-top incentive program at an exotic locale. The special events industry is a world where guests ride elephants through the jungle to their evening's meal (perhaps at the local zoo closed to host the event, or at a themed "jungle" dinner at a hotel or in Bali); dine in the desert, on a mountaintop, on the beach or even in the ocean under a canopy of stars listening a symphony orchestra; enjoy the magic of a private indoor firework display while being served a sump-tuous supper; have Cirque perform a show designed exclusively for them; enjoy private performances by top-name entertainment on a tented rooftop; take pleasure from a custom dancing water display set to music in a private mansion; dine and dance on an acrylic-covered pool that has been set up just for them; savor a candlelit gourmet dinner surrounded by thousands of oak wine casks; watch juggling and dancing fire performers and fabulous custom fire sculptures; have their breath taken away by incredible technology special effects; or take part in an exclusive yacht regatta or road rally crafted just for them. Guests come to the party prepared to expect the unexpected, knowing they will be captivated and enchanted wherever the venue and whatever the theme, no matter the budget or if it is taking place down the street or around the world. Being dazzled and delighted, under the guise of doing business, is a big part of the game being played from Miami to the beaches of Mexico all the way to Mauritius and back.

Confessions of an Event Planner takes readers on an event planning journey around the world and brings the missing event planning element—on-site event execution—to life in a very new way. It is an informative and fun read on its own and allows readers to interact with the book and determine what their course of action would have been should they be party to a similar set of circumstances unfolding before their (sometimes greatly alarmed but never showing it) eyes once you add into the mix the unknown component—the actual invited guests and their personalities. You can plan, you can prepare, you can anticipate and have a backup plan, but crisis mode management is something event planners, corporate and social clients, event suppliers, and venues have to be aware of. They need to be fully apprised of how they should personally and professionally handle the expected and the unexpected.

The game of business travel and special events is one most recently seen acted out in world headlines with rising white-collar arrests. At Tyco CEO Dennis Kozlowski's trial for corporate looting, Kozlowski was accused of charging to Tyco a portion of the $2 million birthday bash—on a Greek island with company executives wearing togas—held for Kozlowski's second wife in 2001. This example is still relevant today, as are further real-life examples laid out in the book, because it shows that corporate clients, as well as their guests, can go out of control and create ethical and legal issues for event planning companies that event planners must be trained to handle and bring to the attention of event planning company heads and their lawyers before a corporate event allowed to run unrestrained by unscrupulous business heads ends up with them in court. There are many examples for event planning companies to study and set company policies from, such as the alleged corporate misspending of company funds by Conrad Black. This time the setting was Bali and a birthday celebration for his wife where board members were in attendance. Were these business affairs attended by corporate execs and paid for in part by the company, or personal parties being paid for out of company funds by the company president? Event planning companies need to know their position and how to protect themselves when asked to do events that bend or break ethical and legal lines.

Being a master of discretion is a major requirement of a corporate and social event planner's job, which can include being privy to sexual romps, financial shenanigans, ethical breaches and eyebrow-raising behavior by corporate execs—such as the recent example that was showcased in newspapers, shown on television and flashed around the Internet of company executives hiring strippers to perform lap dances and topless cart duties at a private corporate golfing tournament. Knowing what to do and how to handle unexpected happenings on location (during site inspections, event advance and when the program is running) to adhere to company policy and procedure and protecting themselves, their company, their clients and their guests from legal ramifications is of paramount importance. Note that in the age of YouTube, etc., corporate shenanigans can backfire more easily than ever.

Confessions of an Event Planner will help individuals as well as companies—event planning and corporations (both for profit and nonprofit)—establish their company's event planning personal and professional A B Cs (A = Anticipation, B = Backup Plan, C = Crisis Mode Management/Code of Conduct) and help them to set company policy, procedure and protocol. *Masters of*

Discretion will have relevance to readers of the entire *Event Plan-ning* suite of books and *The Executive Guide* and move them from creative, strategic and tactical thinking into "real life" prac-tical thinking. Each chapter of the book covers areas of event design (program layout), strategic thinking, guest safety and security, business etiquette, business ethics, time management and more—all topics discussed in the *Event Planning* series and *The Executive Guide,* as well as in my two wedding planners for the professional and consumer market: *Your Stress-Free Wedding Planner: Experts' Best Secrets to Creating the Wedding of Your Dreams* (Sourcebooks, Inc., 2004) and *Plan a Great Wedding in 3 Months or Less* (Sourcebooks, Inc., 2007). These other books will serve as additional training and educational reference guides and as ongoing valuable companion resources to this book, as will the staging and creative life experience design examples that can be found on my website—www.sensualhomeliving.com—and will encompass *Sensual Home Living*™, *Sensual Living for Two*™, *Sensual Suite(s)*™, *Welationship(s)*™ *Building Timeouts for Two*™ *Activities,* *Wecation(s)*™ *Timeouts for Two*™. On my website, I will teach event planners how to transform and change the energy of a room using my trademark design principles and how to create an environment and a life experience for participants that will evoke specific emotions and target all of their senses.

Following is an overview of my other books on event planning and related issues which you may find helpful. *Event Planning: The Ultimate Guide to Successful Meetings, Corporate Events, Fund-Raising Galas, Conferences, Conventions, Incentives and Other Special Events,* Second Edition (Wiley 2009). Any event you plan and stage is a reflection of your organization's image—from the initial invitation to on-site operations. Whether you're planning a product launch, conference, sales meeting, incentive event, or gala fund-raiser, remember that the magic of a truly memorable event is in the details, but so is the devil. Whether your event is for 50 or 2,000 people, whether it has a budget of a few thousand dollars

or hundreds of thousands, it has to be perfect. Fully revised and updated, *Event Planning* gives you a blueprint for planning and executing special events with flair and without any unexpected surprises and expenses. This unique book is loaded with practical advice on:

- Choosing the best venue
- Preparing and managing the budget, with sample costing forms included
- Scheduling, staffing and collaborating with other related professionals
- Coordinating food and beverage, decor, entertainment and themes

The second edition of this book is still the comprehensive guide that it always has been, but with much changing in the industry in recent years, this new edition of *Event Planning* includes:

- Changes in security planning since 9/11
- Innovations in technology and how they can improve—or ruin—an event
- How to stage an environmentally friendly event
- Event risk assessment—what you need to consider before contracting
- How to keep your budget on target and where to find hidden surcharges
- Ways to ease airport stress and make air travel a pleasurable part of the participant's event experience
- When and where event planners and their suppliers will need work visas
- What you need to include in your client's event history in order to design your next event so that it maximizes your client's return on their event investment

- New and updated examples and case studies of where things went right—and wrong
- A companion website with downloadable versions of the checklists, additional forms and tools, author Q&A and more at www.wiley.ca/go/event_planning

What you don't know or know to ask can have a major effect on the success of your event and on your budget. *Event Planning* takes you behind the scenes and through every aspect of organizing and executing a successful event: the planning stages, timing and logistics, budget preparation, operations and on-site management, providing practical tools for anyone who has to plan and execute a truly special event:

- Corporate in-house event planners
- Public relations and communications companies and their clients
- Marketing and corporate communications professionals
- Fund-raisers and not-for-profit organizations
- Professionals in the hospitality and entertainment industries
- Business professionals in charge of planning and handling their company's events

This book will give readers of *Confessions of an Event Planner* a solid foundation of event design principles and clear direction of what to include in each event element to enhance the guest experience.

The Business of Event Planning: Behind-the-Scenes Secrets of Successful Special Events (Wiley, 2002) takes event planning to the next level. Its comprehensive coverage includes strategic event design; how to prepare winning proposals and how to understand them if you're the client; how to determine management fees and negotiate contracts; guest safety and security issues that need to be

taken into consideration; how to design events in multicultural settings; new technology that makes event operations more efficient;
practical tools such as sample letters of agreement, sample layouts
for client proposals, forms, tips and checklists; and a detailed case
study that runs throughout the book—one company that is organizing two very different events. *The Business of Event Planning*
will show you the behind-the-scenes tasks you need to take care
of in your own event planning business before you even plan an
event, and how to take your event design and execution skills to
the next level. This book will show readers of *Confessions of an
Event Planner* how to strategically design and stage both an event
element and a room for targeted results.

*Event Planning Ethics and Etiquette: A Principled Approach
to the Business of Special Event Management* (Wiley, 2003) covers
the business side of event planning ethics, etiquette, entertaining,
acceptable codes of conduct and industry standards. The book provides event planners with the information they need to stay out
of trouble, keep professional relationships healthy and profitable,
avoid the riskier temptations of the lifestyle and win business in
a highly competitive market using ethical business practices. Har-
vard Business School said this book "is a must-read not only for
event professionals, but also for small-business people conceiv-
ing product introductions and conference appearances." This book
will bring important event planning industry business entertaining, business ethics and business etiquette issues to *Confessions of
an Event Planner* readers.

*Marketing Your Event Planning Business: A Creative Ap-
proach to Gaining the Competitive Edge* (Wiley, 2004) takes readers
through marketability, market development and marketing endeav-
ors (business and personal). Topics covered include diversifying
the client base, developing niche markets and areas of expertise,
establishing a backup plan for use during downturns and finding
innovative ways to solicit new sales. This book will show readers

of *Confessions of an Event Planner* how to develop their brand, build customer loyalty and market themselves and their company both in the corporate boardroom and on-site.

Time Management for Event Planners: Expert Techniques and Time-Saving Tips for Organizing Your Workload, Prioritizing Your Day, and Taking Control of Your Schedule (Wiley, 2005) offers expert insight on time management as it relates specifically to the event planning and hospitality industry. Event planning is a high-pressure, around-the-clock job where planners juggle multiple tasks and work down to the wire against crushing deadlines and a mountain of obstacles. For smooth event implementation, and for business success, it is essential that planners manage their own time as expertly as they manage an event. This book illustrates how to do just that. It shows *Confessions of an Event Planner* readers how to create order in their personal and professional time commitments and bring balance into their lives at home and while traveling for business and pleasure.

The Executive's Guide to Corporate Events and Business Entertaining: How to Choose and Use Corporate Functions to Increase Brand Awareness, Develop New Business, Nurture Customer Loyalty and Drive Growth (Wiley, 2007). The primary focus of this book is the strategic event marketing thinking from a business objective perspective, not just an event planning one, and will give business executives—who are now being held accountable for event results—insight on how to choose, design and use events to achieve business objectives and how to generate a return on their company's investment of time and money. As well, design elements and strategies found in this book will give event planners the tools they need to understand how the events they plan can better meet multiple layers of corporate objectives. This book will give event planners the ability to see the event from their client's perspective as well as an event planning perspective. Executing events flawlessly does not mean that corporate goals are

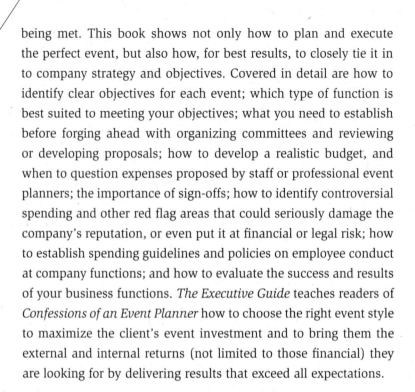

being met. This book shows not only how to plan and execute the perfect event, but also how, for best results, to closely tie it in to company strategy and objectives. Covered in detail are how to identify clear objectives for each event; which type of function is best suited to meeting your objectives; what you need to establish before forging ahead with organizing committees and reviewing or developing proposals; how to develop a realistic budget, and when to question expenses proposed by staff or professional event planners; the importance of sign-offs; how to identify controversial spending and other red flag areas that could seriously damage the company's reputation, or even put it at financial or legal risk; how to establish spending guidelines and policies on employee conduct at company functions; and how to evaluate the success and results of your business functions. *The Executive Guide* teaches readers of *Confessions of an Event Planner* how to choose the right event style to maximize the client's event investment and to bring them the external and internal returns (not limited to those financial) they are looking for by delivering results that exceed all expectations.

Special note: The event planning case stories captured blog-style are based on true but fictionalized events, and actual names, locations, programs as they took place and companies have not been used.

Judy Allen

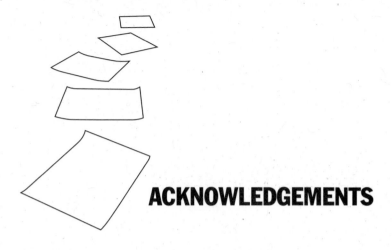

ACKNOWLEDGEMENTS

Over the course of seven years, because of reader response for the first edition of *Event Planning: The Ultimate Guide* and requests from planners-to-be, planners working in the field and business professionals for more event planning answers, *Event Planning: The Ultimate Guide* grew into a best-selling series of business books that are being used around the world by industry professionals and corporate executives as well as universities and colleges for course adoption and required reading. The books have now been translated into five languages.

This well-received series of books then became the crossover platform for two mass-market consumer books—with more to come. My first wedding planning guide led the way in wedding planning category sales and received media reviews, deeming the wedding planner to be one of the best wedding planners on the market because of its event planning focus.

Confessions of an Event Planner returns me to the event planning realm. It came into being as a direct result of readers' queries as to how to handle situations on-site that no one had prepared them for and how to protect themselves from legal and ethical repercussions from actions they were privy to both in corporate boardrooms and resort guest bedrooms.

I would like to thank my publisher, John Wiley, for bringing this book out to serve as a full-circle teaching tool that embraces the entire suite of *Event Planning* books.

I would like to thank the outstanding professionals at John Wiley & Sons Canada, Ltd. for their contribution to the making of this book and express my appreciation to Robert Harris, General Manager; Bill Zerter, COO; Jennifer Smith, Vice President and Publisher; Elizabeth McCurdy, Project Manager; Kimberly Rossetti, Senior Coordinator, Editorial & Special Projects; Deborah Guichelaar, Publicist; Erin Kelly, Publicity Manager; Erika Zupko, Publicity Coordinator; Lucas Wilk, Marketing Manager; Adrian So, Senior Graphics Designer; Pauline Ricablanca, Project Coordinator; Brian Will, Editorial Assistant; Meghan Brousseau, New Media and Rights Manager; Jessica Ting, Accounting and Royalty Manager; Stacey Clark, Corporate Sales Manager.

I would like to say a special thank-you to Karen Milner, Executive Editor, whose vision and direction opened the door to this series coming into being. She suggested that I expand the original concept I had for the first book to encompass all of my event planning knowledge and areas of expertise that came from designing one-of-a-kind special events in more than 30 countries and the incredible opportunity of working with some amazingly talented people in the special event industry.

I have truly enjoyed working with Michelle Bullard on the structure and copyedit of my books. Michelle challenges me constantly to go further in order to bring to *Event Planning* readers the maximum amount of wisdom I can share. Having worked with me on the majority of my event planning books, Michelle is a master at catching me when I slip into industry language without detailing or showing what I mean by example. Her trained eye is one of the best, and the questions she poses to me are very relevant to making a better book.

I would also like to thank everyone who has reviewed my books and provided such positive comments and feedback. I greatly appreciate the time you have given to me and to my readers by reviewing this book. Your opinions are greatly valued by all of us.

I had the opportunity to write this book as well as the second edition of *Event Planning: The Ultimate Guide* in the wonderful "active living" town of Collingwood, Ontario. I wish to repeat my thank-yous to some very special people who came into my life while I was living there:

- Sarah Applegarth MSc, CSCS, CSEP-CEP, SCS, Strength & Conditioning Coach, Active Life Conditioning Inc. (www.activelifeconditioning.com), whose business is "Taking Care of What Matters Most—You." Sarah is a world-class high-performance trainer and someone I was privileged enough to call my personal trainer when I turned to her for expert help in an area that I had no knowledge in and needed her expertise in learning how to develop the physical, mental and emotional strength, stamina and flexibility athletes carry at their core to become their best so that they can do more, give more and bring their best to themselves, their family, their friends, their work (life purpose) and the world.
- Brianne Law, World Cup coach for the Canadian Para-Alpine Ski Team (www.canski.org), who joined Sarah in training me this past summer, and is an amazing trainer and teacher.
- Krista Campbell, Registered Massage Therapist, my massage therapist who is trained in Swedish massage techniques and whose amazing healing touch had my muscles back moving as they are meant to.
- Dr. Heather Munroe, Chiropractor, Mountain Chiropractic (www.mountainchiropractic.ca), who in just one session was able to undo the damage a fall had done and brought me back to pain-free alignment, and then went on to release years of joint compression caused by years of sitting behind a computer, sitting in an airplane and sitting in meetings around the world.

In my book *Time Management for Event Planners*, I shared the importance of having personal and professional balance in life and the value of taking part in all life experiences that present themselves in order to elevate your level of knowledge and creativity. I shared all that I had learned but did not address the area of physical well-being, as it was a life-learning, life-challenging, life-changing and growing experience that was still to come. It came about from having a business partner who is a seven times Ironman who honors his commitment to physical well-being no matter where he is in the world or what his day personally and professionally demands, as do Sarah, Brianne, Krista and Heather—my well-being immersion "pit fit team"—and their life partners.

Living in an active living community for a year with people committed to health and well-being and surrounded by nature has been an incredible journey and one I am grateful to have experienced. I have learned that there is an amazing benefit to living an active lifestyle at home, at work and as you travel around the world on site inspections, fam trips and on-site programs; to being fueled by nurturing and nourishing foods and fitness workouts, not just caffeine and meals on the run when they can be fit in between work deadlines and demands that can be intensive in this 24/7 industry; and to bringing wellness, fitness and health lifestyle elements into not only your everyday and work life but the programs that you design so that others can experience the benefits.

I would also like to thank Judith Somborac, Personal Direction, Training and Coaching, my yoga and Pilates trainer; and Jackey Fox, Assistant Manager, A&P. Each played an important part in my fitness mission to counteract years of sitting at the computer and taught me about nutrition, stamina, strength and stretching—literally, not just physically—as a tool to push past discomfort in all areas of life. They shared their talents and expert knowledge with me, giving me new tools I can use every day for the rest of my life while I take on the world and the world of possibilities in front of me personally and professionally through my company, 2jproductions, with Joe Shane. I am excited to gain a new sense of purpose, passion and play that is bringing me closer to my personal, professional (life purpose) and creative best.

I would like to say a very special thank-you to Ysabelle Allard, Bilingual Meetings & Incentives (Toronto), whom I came to know through my first event planning book, *Event Planning: The Ultimate Guide,* and with whom I share a deep affection for the island of Barbados. Ysabelle is directly responsible for a move that will take me into the next chapter of my life. I appreciate her friendship and all that knowing her has brought to me. Sometimes, in some areas, we are teachers, and sometimes, in other areas, we are students with the right teachers having been placed in our path to move us in the direction we are meant to go and grow in. As you grow in awakening and awareness, it gets easier to recognize special people coming into your life for a reason. Both Ysabelle and my business partner and beloved friend Joe Shane came into my life through my writing my first book. Life is an interesting journey that can be lived as a special event when you let it unfold as it is meant to without self-imposed roadblocks and resistance.

I would like to thank my incredible new trainer in Barbados, Levar Greaves, who works out of Surfside Wellness Centre and Surfside Fitness Centre and who is known for "breaking barriers"— physical, mental and emotional—and who is taking me to a new level of active living, one that embraces a sense of play as well as perfect workout form. And Natasha and Mike Mahy, dive shop Reefers and Wreckers owner, and their son, Oscar, whose apartment I am renting during my stay in Barbados—with added thanks to Ysabelle for the part she played in bringing this about. It's the perfect setting and location for working out, writing, working on a new website for Joe and me, and several design projects.

As always, I would like to thank my family—my parents, Walter and Ruth; my sister, Marilyn, and my brother-in-law, Hans; and

my nieces and their partners: Natasha and her husband, Ed, and their much loved new baby Gillian, and Jasmine and Rodney—and my friends for their continued love and support.

And again, I would like to say thank you to my 2jproductions partner, Joe Shane. I look forward to working with you on taking event planning to an exciting, creative and innovative new level. There is no one I would want to take this journey with more than you.

PROFILE

Name: Emma (Em) Starr **Age:** Thirty-something

Gender: Female **Marital Status:** Divorced

Location: Always somewhere different—or on my way there

Occupation: Owner and Creative Director of Starr Productions, a boutique event management company that specializes in designing, producing and orchestrating corporate and high-profile social and celebrity events around the world.

Favorite Things: Family; friends; travel; photography; snorkelling; kick boxing; strength and resistance training; Pilates; biking; horseback riding; exploring new (preferably warm) destinations; shopping for one-of-a-kind finds; clothes made from natural fabrics; writing in my journal; dining out or room service; dancing under the stars; walking the beach in Barbados, Hawaii, the South Pacific, Greece, the Maldives; or hiking through the woods; romping with my dogs; doing yoga on the beach by the lake at home; staying in six- and seven-star hotels; flying first class or in private planes; being pampered; convertibles; luxury linens; spicy food; fine wines and champagne; being first to create something new; making meaningful and magical memories for others to enjoy; being successful in business

Least Favorite Things: Cooking, cleaning, shopping malls with their cookie-cutter clothes, roughing it and playing sports (I'd much rather be the official photographer and cheerleader)

Favorite Quote: Your life is the ultimate special event—design it with care." —*Emma Starr*

Favorite Music: Mixed; everything from Sade and Keiko Matsui to pop, calypso and reggae

Favorite Movies: Classic movies from the 40s, 50s, 60s and 70s, but I stay on top of today's hits

Favorite Television Shows: Reality shows like *The Amazing Race* and *Survivor*, in which show components are very similar to corporate events with team and individual challenges

Favorite Books to Read: Professionally, bestsellers to keep tabs on the mood of today and what could be the next cutting-edge theme or hot trend; and personally, books that educate and enlighten, that challenge my mind, body and soul to grow

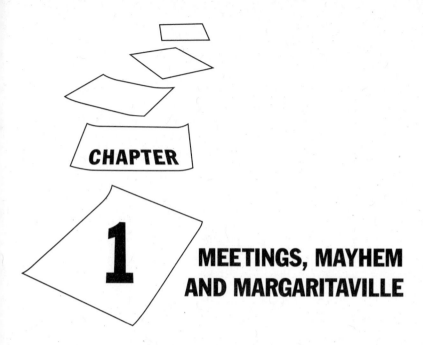

CHAPTER

1

MEETINGS, MAYHEM AND MARGARITAVILLE

Em finds herself in a distressing real-life situation that tests her ability to walk the fine event planning line of giving her clients what they want and keeping their guests safe, as they spiral out of control on an all-male incentive getaway reward for top sales that would turn into an event planner's worst nightmare of "guests gone wild."

DECEMBER 13

What a day it's been! Started out the same as most arrival days, with "they're herrrrrrrre"—à la *Poltergeist*—echoing through my mind as soon as I learned the plane had touched down. I knew I was minutes away from experiencing another round of "some things have to be seen to be believed." I know the actual phrase is "some things have to be believed to be seen" but in my case I *know* the opposite is true. What takes place under the premise of business is entertaining to say the least, guaranteed to raise an eyebrow or two and sometimes my blood pressure, and today did exactly that.

It began with my airport arrival team calling to let me know that all 50 men were present and accounted for but . . . and I have

learned to hold my breath when I hear the "but" and today was no different . . . they are in very high spirits and already spinning out of control. It was a huge mistake to have them all fly down together on the same plane. It's something we never recommend, because should disaster strike a whole company's top executives and their top performers could be wiped out in an instant. Since 9/11, many corporations have put travel policies in effect for this very reason. But, it was what their company wanted—their whole top sales force partying in the aisles, celebrating their recent successes on their way down to the company meeting. And a young, all-male sales force, traveling with no spouses or significant others to rein them in, with a free open bar and lots of corporate encouragement, knows how to "get their crunk on and wile out," as this group likes to say. Trying to outdo one another will be a given. The very nature of their business is competition and a sales force is high energy at the best of times. I know we are going to have our hands full 24/7. So much for chilling out in Margaritaville.

As soon as I heard that the party had begun, I gave the hotel manager a mayhem alert. I knew that the hotel's poor guests would have no idea what was going to hit them about 15 minutes after I sounded the alert. I knew that their tranquility bubble was about to burst.

Pop! Sheer horror is the best way to describe the expressions on both hotel staff and guest faces alike when our rowdy crowd of men spilled out of the motor coaches and into the lobby, dancing and singing on their way to their private check-in. The company chose this hotel because it was self-contained, out of the way and removed from the temptations of downtown. They wanted to keep their meeting attendees from straying too far, having taken over half of the guestrooms in the hotel and pretty much all of the function space for private meetings and parties. The hotel's guests, on the other hand, had selected this vacation spot for an idyllic week away from noisy intrusion. They began craning their necks to see what all the noise was about as soon as the motor coach arrived. I could see that they were hoping against hope that this was merely a pit stop for the group and they would soon be on their way to town to stay at another hotel. The hotel staff, however, knew better.

I hated to shatter the hotel guests' momentary glimmer of hope but it was time for lights, camera and action, and with a discreet motion I had my program directing team move in for the official meet and greet. Having been forewarned as to the group's general condition, we had already advised the bartenders, standing at the ready with the welcome margaritas and beer, to go light on the alcohol and not be too quick at filling requests for beer. Dee Dee, lead event director extraordinaire, was already circulating and encouraging "the guys" to sample some of the food—high in protein and carbs to sop up the alcohol, and with little salt (no nuts, pretzels or chips) as we didn't want to encourage further drinking—that had been laid out to buffer the effects of what for many obviously had been a liquid lunch.

I have traveled the world with Dee Dee and there is no one else I would rather have beside me on-site when doing a program. I have watched her work the room using her magic, getting others to do her bidding with her gentle, coaxing way. Little did people know that under that outer layer of genteelness lay five feet two inches of pure determination and what Dee Dee referred to as her "spicy Latina temper," which caused her dark eyes to go from warm and welcoming to flashing warning signals in an instant if anyone or anything came up on program that would challenge our ability to deliver a flawless event while under her expert direction. Those who had encountered her displeasure with their actions knew to tread carefully in future encounters. I always knew that whatever had to be done would be done, right and on time, if assigned to Dee Dee. She had no patience for people who gave less than their personal and professional best. Dee Dee often says, "don't ask me

how but it will get done" and it always is—sometimes by temporarily ruffling feathers in her quest for the best.

When you are running a live production, which is what a special event is, you don't get a second chance to make things right or even do a dress rehearsal. It's live, baby, live. My company and staff's reputation, my client's reputation and corporate or social image, thousands of dollars—sometimes hundreds of thousands to millions of client dollars—are all on the line. Messing up the part we play in putting all the pieces together from design to on-site orchestration is not an option. Unfortunately, that doesn't apply in reverse. Cleaning up the messes my clients and their guests have been known to make when they are permitted to run amok (translated to guests, company execs and their employees gone wild) with and without my client's blessing is an entirely different matter and an expected part of the job. From the looks of it, we're going to have a lively time this week keeping ahead of this crew, including the corporate executives.

The company heads *loved* all the testosterone let loose in the room, actively encouraging their sales staff's hijinks and setting the tone for their stay. They want them revved up, ready to hit the sales floor running when they get back to the office, anxious to achieve sales goals so they can be a part of the next company getaway. It's one of their main objectives this week. And they want the ones who didn't meet their targets and were left behind to wish they had been a part of the fun and festivities, and double their efforts so they can be part of this elite group (within their company) next time a round. Envy can be a powerful motivator.

Making sure that those who qualified to come have an unforgettable time is what we do. We are also responsible, in part, for making sure the guests return home in one piece, with no injuries, arrests or other incidents to mar their time away, but those in my industry know that's not always possible. Some attendees, as well as those responsible for hosting their events, have ended up being fired on the spot, involved in fist fights, thrown into jail, packed up and moved out of the hotel they were staying in, escorted to the airport to be put on the plane home, ended up divorced, become the talk of their industry and sometimes, as we have seen lately, making headlines that have been flashed around the world via the media and the Internet. Being wined and dined to the nth degree, in a staged air of casual camaraderie, can sometimes make it possible for invited guests to forget they are attending a business function or social event put on by a company who at the end of the day has an image to uphold. It's easy for personal and professional lines to get blurred when unlimited alcohol is involved and you are far away from home traveling on business in an exotic locale, staying in five-, six- and seven-star resorts and not necessarily with your spouse or significant other along. Anything and everything you can imagine does take place. It's our job to remain on high alert, diffuse any potentially dangerous situations and turn down the dial on excess frolicking before it gets out of control, doing it all with the utmost of discretion.

I was aware from the very beginning that we may need to revise some plans to avoid things going awry. I called a quick huddle with company execs to suggest a change but always, always away from guests and hotel staff. Being masters of discretion is part of our modus operandi.

The original plans called for the corporate hospitality suite to be open for drinks, mixing and mingling during the afternoon, but after a quick conference with company heads I was able to convince them that it would be better for all to slow down the pace as we still had the evening ahead. Tomorrow they have a full day of meetings to attend and it would not be in anyone's best interest to find their participants not fit to take part, having shown up wasted or hungover. Time to rein in the fun for the moment. The guests had no idea that an open hospitality suite had been planned so they didn't miss it. It was time for them to relax, settle in, swim,

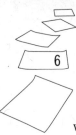

work out or take a nap so that they could be refreshed for the evening ahead. It also gave my staff time to grab something to eat and a chance to regroup, and for those of us who had come down several days ahead of the group, to meet with the hotel and other suppliers and prep the group arrival, and to be filled in on what took place on the flight down and on the transfer to the hotel.

It's no joke that it's important going into any program to be able to identify whom we'll need to pay special attention. Someone will end up wearing the title of Head Instigator and Chief Mischief Maker. There's always at least one on every program, no matter what profession or industry the guests are from. Lawyers, stockbrokers, auto manufacturers and car dealership owners, pharmaceutical, retail, real estate, manufacturing, entertainment—they all have "the one" you know you are going to have your hands full managing. And sometimes it's the company president, CEO, company executives or their staff. Who'll it be this time? I don't know yet, but it's only a matter of time.

Then there's Mr. or Ms. Amorous to contend with, who thinks sleeping with the event planning staff is part of the package. Thank heavens I learned early who to watch out for . . . and for the buddy system we have in place. None of us is ever left alone with any kind of creep—placed in a compromising situation or fending off an unwanted advance. Any such situation is easily circumvented once you know who to watch out for. The case where a well-known athlete had a young female hotel staff member step inside his room and then closed the door behind her should serve as a warning as to why you should never step into someone's bedroom suite alone or without the door left wide open, but some people learn the hard way. In that case, the hotel employee said she had been raped. Her hotel had a policy of making sure that the hotel door was left open when stepping into a guest's room for that very reason. It protects both the hotel staff member and the hotel guest from accusations and applies equally to other guests visiting other guests' rooms, Your personal and professional reputation can be irreparably ruined in a matter of minutes by one lapse of judgment, and in this business it can become easily clouded by being starstruck, having too much to drink or simply a desire to please, or being too trusting and totally forgetting the situation you could find yourself in. Knowing who to be on guard around is imperative in this job in order to be proactive in finessing and sidestepping tricky ethical and even legal situations.

And we can't forget Mr. or Ms. Entitlement, who believes their every whim should be catered to. Not that they're any kind of VIP or anything, but they sure think they are. Those "you don't know who you're talking to" types. The kind who demand to be upgraded on the sly to the hotel's presidential suite. Umm, don't think so. The room assignments are not done by chance but rather are the express choice of the company head hosting their event. The truth is that if Mr. or Ms. Entitlement do not think they are being accommodated in a room that reflects their social or company stature, neither we nor the hotel staff are the ones who allocated that room to them but of course you can't say or even allude to that fact. One of the instructions the rooms manager receives is that the hotel or resort cannot change the room assignment without consulting us first. There is a pecking order. If through overbooking we must make upgrades, they aren't done based on a whim or on a guest's wishes. In some cases, the client may prefer to have any upgrades assigned to Mr. and Mrs. Joe Public rather than have their guests in different room categories. Every group is different, but what needs to be done in these kinds of situations is worked out months in advance. Mr. and Ms. Entitlement are easily recognized from calls they have made to the office beforehand with their various requests, but closet Mr. and Ms. Entitlements do show up on-site. They're usually the first ones back at the hospitality desk after they have been up to see their room and completed their mission to compare it to what others in the group have been checked into.

Last week we made a fun wager on who we believe will be first back to the desk.

Mr. Macho and Ms. Thong (sometimes Mr. Thong) are also among the other personalities that often show up on-site. Oh goody.

The majority of guests are sweethearts, but it only takes one out-of-control guest to ruin it for the rest. And it's our job to stop that from happening. Savvy and skilled program directors use the ABC principles of event planning (A=Anticipation, B=Backup Plan, C=Code of Conduct), which varies from client to client, guest to guest, to handle situations that crop up so that they don't have to kick into crisis management mode. Being able to read people and their personality types makes it easier to deal with situations as they come up. As an experienced program director I'm usually doing back-to-back business, social and celebrity events around the world for every type of client under the sun, and there's very little I haven't seen, done or handled.

I watched as, room keycards in hand, the guys started to head into the hotel in search of their guestroom. To help tone things down, they have not been given private rooms but are sharing a room with one of their colleagues. This didn't apply to the company heads, though. The pairing—who was sharing with whom—was strategically planned so that certain individuals would get to spend quality time one on one with someone the company hoped they would bond with, share sales techniques with and discuss common challenges with over the course of their stay—and keep tabs on them. Fifty men came down and we must have all of them present and accounted for at the end of their stay. And the general consensus from the get-go was that there would be less room for inhibitions to run free if they were paired with a roommate. But then again, if the company heads have made the wrong match, we could end up with double the trouble on our hands. The dynamics of every group are different; however, I'm used to getting a mix of people from different social spheres, education backgrounds, and life and business experiences.

But, back to my recap of today. From all the hooting, whooo hoooing and laughter coming from the balconies, it was no secret that the top sales staff had discovered the 80-gallon Jacuzzis in their two- and three-bedroom suites and were busy discussing in-room party possibilities. Everyone had tried to earn the Jacuzzi suites, which would no doubt soon be "party central." We'd assigned all the guestrooms to the same general area to try to keep the noise contained, but with this crowd? Doubt that's possible. They're here for a good time and will be going full blast. In minutes they were back down, hanging out at the tiki bar, roughhousing in the junior Olympic-size heated swimming pool, taking note of the tropical garden setting and checking out the fitness center, while sending some of the others on a quest to find the nearest place to stock up on beer and snacks for their rooms. And yes, just like clockwork, this group's Mr. Entitlement has already shown up at the hospitality desk, wanting to be assigned to a room with a Jacuzzi as well. It didn't seem to matter to him that he didn't qualify to be in one. Sighhhh. I left him in Dee Dee's capable hands and headed out to advance dinner preparations. Sorry, Dee Dee!

Tonight was just what I was hoping for—very low-key. Everyone had a long travel day with an early morning flight and a connection through Miami. With the drinking and being out in the sun, after coming from winter weather, they were toasted in more ways than one and ready to retire early tonight. A simple welcome reception and dinner is the general rule of thumb for planning first-night activities. No use spending major dollars when guests, no matter how much they want to let loose, will be headed to bed early. Some didn't even make it down to dinner tonight! They have a full day of meetings tomorrow and dinner off-property in the evening. By then they will have gotten their second wind, feeding off

each other's energy and gathering in groups to create mischief—Day Two is what we're bracing for.

Didn't really need to open the corporate hospitality suite this evening. Those who did show up were starting to fade by the time the Key Lime Pie was being served. Most were missing in action, fast asleep, their roommates told us. A parting announcement by company heads was made letting their guys know that early morning wake-up calls had been scheduled on their behalf to make sure everyone was present for the group breakfast, and that while they wanted everyone to have a great time, being late for their meeting was not an option.

Finally, it was time for us to turn in and call it a night as well.

DECEMBER 14

My 4:00 a.m. wake-up call came in on schedule. We were off to a good start. First things first. I called down to the front desk to see if anything went amiss last night. Everything was *fairly*—there was emphasis on the *fairly*—quiet last night. Good. That means shenanigans may have gone on but nothing to be overly concerned with as yet.

Our day always starts well in advance of the group. We had the hospitality desk to set up, notices to post, breakfast preparations to oversee, meeting room setup to approve, audiovisual equipment to test out and a hundred other items to cross off our function sheets, the bible for on-site program directors and event planning suppliers and venues. Everything that has to be done and the manner in which it is to be performed is laid out on those sheets. Each event element is scripted, carefully laid out minute by minute so that everyone involved with the program is operating with the same information and all know exactly what is expected from them. We ensure our function sheets are crafted with military precision and timing. Movie and stage directors have it easy; they can do endless rehearsals or say cut and shoot the scene over again. For me, there's no safety net. My function sheets have to be perfect, and for an intricate program that might mean a hundred pages of perfection. They are sent out in advance to all involved, who review and rework them before going out on the "pre-con"— the pre-event walk-through of the function sheets with staff, venue and suppliers before the event takes place. Function sheets get everyone on the same page, even if the person who's orchestrating the event on-site isn't the one I began the planning process with. Let's face it . . . I don't have time to deal with people who aren't up to speed, and there's little room for error. Holding a pre-con to review the function sheets makes sure those who will be on-site have read them and there are no misconceptions as to what is and is not included and how it is to be done.

I usually like to get up early enough to take a few moments for myself by the ocean whenever I am staying at a beachfront location. To me, watching the sunrise, taking a dip or doing yoga by the water is one of my favorite perks of the job. After that, I was off to shower, change into "work" clothes and get ready to meet Dee Dee for coffee before we started our rounds. I wouldn't dream of running around in a bathing suit or yoga wear once clients or even hotel staff are up and about. If trip directors have scheduled time off during the day, arrangements are made for them to use another's hotel's beach and pool facilities. It's just better to maintain a polished, professional look around guests and hotel employees at all times. Lounging around the hotel pool or on the beach in a bikini or even a more conservative bathing suit sends the wrong message even if it is on my off time.

Breakfast ready to go. Check.

Meeting room set up as requested. Check.

Audiovisual working. Check.

Dee Dee is overseeing breakfast and the other program directors are at the hospitality desk ready to answer any questions the
corporate heads or their guests may have. They will also call—
should it be necessary—the rooms of any missing attendees who
don't get up for breakfast to make sure they're on their way. I hope
everyone answers their phone so we don't have to send hotel staff
to check on them.

Today will actually be pretty light. The guys will have breakfast
and be in meetings most of the day. They'll break for mid-morning
refreshments and a barbecue lunch, but each time they'll immediately head back into the meeting room. Only sweet tea, lemonade
and sodas will be served with lunch. Against my reservations, the
corporate hospitality suite will open once the meeting is finished
and then it's off for a night on the town as a group. This is party
night and the corporate execs want them wound up from the moment the meeting lets out. I am certain it is going to be a very long
and very late night.

■   ■   ■

The guys are starting to surface and many of them look a little worse
for wear. Too much sun, too much drinking and too little sleep will
do it every time. They are very subdued right now—nothing like the
group that arrived. But experience has taught us they will bounce
back and often with a vengeance. I've asked Dee Dee to monitor the
meeting room to make sure that it doesn't get too warm. Better to
have it a touch on the cooler side so no one drifts off to sleep during
the session and their attention will not be as likely to wander. The
hospitality desk has been positioned in a way that attendees will not
be tempted to slip out and ditch staying for the full meeting once it
has started. It happens. One client, at their tropical getaway, had one
of their staff assigned to beach duty to make sure they redirected
any lost souls from their group that "mistook" the beach or the pool

as the meeting venue, and the golf course was instructed not to accept any requests for tee-off times from any of their attendees when meetings were taking place. As with most out-of-town and out-of-country meetings that are both business and pleasure, there are tax implications, and companies work hard to make sure that all rules and regulations are met. Records are kept to make sure all is adhered to—and truth be known. some are real and others are fictional.

Some of the stories you hear about the goings-on in this industry never fail to surprise you. One company booked meeting rooms, equipment, breaks and lunches and paid for them, but they were only meetings scheduled for the "books," not for real. Unfortunately for them, they also scheduled a golf tournament and private events to take place at the same time as the supposed meetings, leaving a paper trial that could not be denied. Not a smart move. And asking the hotel and others involved to look the other way placed suppliers in a difficult position and crossed ethical boundaries big time. This is the time I'd lay all my cards on the table and walk away. I'd much rather a client who assigns beach patrol duty. They mean business and not monkey business. But while they work hard when they are away, they also party hard. I'm pretty sure this is what this group will turn out to be like. My team and I are prepared for anything to happen. These guys, while they are dragging their tails right now, are high spirited because of the nature of their work and the type of personality that sales attracts, and they will be flying high by the end of their stay.

■　　　■　　　■

Coffee breaks and lunch went without incident. And the corporate execs met me halfway regarding the afternoon hospitality suite—bartenders were brought in to maintain some semblance of liquor control. I knew there'd be a lot of drinking going on tonight and I

wanted them in relatively good shape before we set out. The extra local staff we have on-site tonight are all men that look like they can handle themselves and anything else that may be thrown at them. They'll be there until the very last guest returns to the hotel, to lend a hand if anyone has more alcohol than they can manage.

And then we were off. Or at least they're off. Dee Dee and I were one step ahead of them, advancing tonight's progressive dinner and drinks party and in constant touch with the rest of our crew via cell phones, PDAs and walkie-talkies. Open-air trains and "go cups" with their choice of alcoholic or non-alcoholic beverage were waiting for the group at the front of the hotel, setting the energy vibe for the evening ahead. The first stop on the route was "sunset celebrations and libations" at a pier made popular for its spectacular sunsets. Private vendors were set up just for the group, with finger food appetizers and drinks for the guys to enjoy while they watched the nightly salute to the sun take place amid musicians, jugglers and street performers. Then it was back on board to the next stop, which was a great seafood and steak restaurant right on the water that's known for its cuisine and fun atmosphere. Tonight the restaurant belonged to the group. As part of the restaurant's seafood display offerings, a live mermaid was sitting among the seafood specialties. I saw that as a potential red flag and assigned Dee Dee to keep a close eye on Ms. Mermaid, even though the owner assured us that no one before had ever made improper advances or given her a difficult time.

You could hear the guys coming before you even saw the open-air train rounding the corner. The early afternoon drinks followed by the "go cups" and sunset drinks had kicked in. Everyone was in great spirits but they'd settled in nicely. Some were placing their food and drink orders and some were helping themselves to the seafood buffet, when uh-oh—they finally discovered the live mermaid and just as I thought, they decided to have some fun. Mr. Instigator decided that it was their duty to set her free and release her back to the ocean and rallied his buddies to come help, which they quickly did. You could see that Ms. Mermaid was getting a little anxious and so was the owner—he finally saw what we had been saying. The distance between where Ms. Mermaid was draped along the table and the drop into the ocean was only a few feet, and with her heavy mermaid tail she would've quickly sunk, not swam away. Dee Dee, some of the male staff members and I were positioned to react quickly and make sure no actual physical harm came to her. We diffused the situation before it escalated to the next level. The advance team then headed off to make sure that everything was ready and waiting at the next progressive stop for local dessert specialties and coffee.

After dessert it was time to hit the bars, including Sloppy Joe's, which has long been associated with Ernest Hemingway, and the Green Parrot, an internationally known bar and a local landmark since 1890. We used this opportunity to introduce the group to a couple of bars they would enjoy if they returned to town on their own or again as a group of 50 guys. We are in a very liberal destination with a live-and-let-live social society and you'll find a mixture of gay and non-gay bars, so we'd researched the best of both during our advance preparations. We'd prepared a list with recommendations for distribution among the guys. Of course, the places where women have been known to leave their inhibitions behind along with their bras and where regulars dance with abandon on tabletops may have been "accidentally" left off the list. We hadn't lost sight of the temptation to smuggle some newfound friends back to the hotel to enjoy the in-room Jacuzzis!

Suddenly—oh my—Mr. Instigator picked up Dee Dee from behind and spun her around over his head, just narrowly missing the ceiling fan. The corporate execs standing nearby laughed at his antics but quickly ordered him to put her down before we moved in.

A conch train stood by to head back to the hotel with anyone wanting to return early. Not surprisingly the conch train sat empty;

no one was ready to call it a night or no one wanted to be seen as the first one to head back to the hotel. The private conch shuttles were scheduled to operate until the bars closed. The group was now on their own with the exception of the local staff, two members of our team and Dee Dee, who would stay till the end. After this point there was no way of really keeping track of who was coming and going. Some will catch a cab on their own and head back when they are ready or take off for parts unknown, returning to the hotel just in time for breakfast. Hopefully, they won't do too much damage to themselves or the town. The rest of the team and I headed back in case anything at the hotel required our attention. For us the night was still very young as much as we might long for bed. The evening so far had been a success. Both the corporate execs and guys were pleased. They got to drink in the sights while drinking in public, take part in a famous sunset ritual and sample local cuisine and the bars. Good times.

■   ■   ■

It's 1:00 a.m. Some of the group are starting to roll in. A few are not too steady on their feet but they seem to be taking care of one another. One was very embarrassed and belligerent but his buddies were calming him down. Apparently, Mr. Instigator thought it would be fun not to let him into the men's room at the bar and he had an accident times two. Dee Dee had let us know what had taken place so we knew what to expect. He had been threatening bodily harm to all that took part in the "prank." One of the men on our staff discreetly offered to have his pants taken away and cleaned with no one the wiser. In expressing his gratitude he burst into tears. He didn't want to bring them home in that condition and have to explain what happened to his family, he said as he flipped open his wallet to show us pictures of his wife and kids. He had been feeling diminished in front of his colleagues and worried that he would become the joke of the office. Thankfully, the friends he had made on the trip had not abandoned him and were not making him feel worse than he already did. Chances are by the end of this week this particular incident will be long forgotten.

■　　■　　■

It's 2:00 a.m. now. Dee Dee and the rest of the team are back but not all of the guys have returned. Dee Dee caught me up on the goings-on after I left and we discussed the number of women that had ended up hanging around and physically off the men. They had to stop more than a few of them from climbing aboard the conch train and returning back to the hotel with the guys who wanted to party, roommate or not, married or not. Then I updated her on Mr. Pranked. We decided that there was not much more we could do right now with regard to those who hadn't come back yet, so it was time for us to head to our beds to catch some sleep if we could.

■　　■　　■

3:05 a.m. Rinngggggggggg. It was the night manager suggesting I come down to handle some situations. I asked if I needed reinforcements and he suggested that it would be a good thing. I called Dee Dee's room and then quickly dressed to scope out what had taken place.

Pool party!!! Ah yes. And with a number of the girls that the guys had picked up at the bars. The guys had broken into the corporate hospitality suite and grabbed some drinks. Bottles were everywhere, as were articles of clothing. Naked pool party!!! Dee Dee happened upon Mr. Instigator about to pour bubble bath into the pool and quickly confiscated it. Hotel security had been summoned as well and were successfully getting both guests and non-guests out of the pool and into their clothes. The visitors had been "smuggled" onto the property with the hotel staff none the wiser—or looking the other way (in the manner of "what happens in Vegas, stays in Vegas")—until the impromptu pool party broke out and something had to be done as other hotel guests were getting annoyed. Chastened and expressing fake remorse, the guys took off to their rooms and cabs were called for the rest, but not before telephone numbers and the like were exchanged.

With the hotel staff capably dealing with the pool cleanup, restoring order to the corporate hospitality suite—it would be re-stocked tomorrow—and calculating the extra charges to be added to the master account, Dee Dee and I said our thank-yous and headed for bed again to grab another hour or so of sleep. For the moment, all seems quiet but we aren't about to let down our guard. I am sure we both fell asleep with one ear open, waiting for the telephone to summon us again.

DECEMBER 15

This morning, the corporate execs laughed at the antics of "their boys." We didn't discuss the specifics of what took place with Mr. Pranked. He didn't want to be shamed in front of his company heads and had asked us not to make his name known and tell them exactly what transpired unless it was absolutely necessary. If we did, we assured him, it would be done with the utmost of discretion and he was not to worry.

The company heads knew there were other incidents that had transpired but at the moment all was under control and they said they preferred to be on a "need to know" basis. If they did not have to bail someone out of jail or take someone to the hospital, they really wanted the guys to have a good time without being reported on or knowing exactly what took place. We did need to make them aware of the happenings at the pool and the hospitality suite break-in—without naming names, as per their request—because extra charges were going to be showing up on the final reconciliation. How, or if, they choose to address this with their staff is entirely up to them. But what they did want was everyone present and accounted for at their meeting, regardless of how rough they felt or how late they got in last night. Dee Dee said it would be her pleasure to personally call those who were missing and make sure they were on time, with a sweet "don't ask me how but I can assure you they will be there." Of that I had no doubt. I felt that she would have a special wake-up call—with my blessing—arranged for Mr. Instigator, who had still not shown up.

■　　■　　■

By 9:00 a.m., everyone was present and thankfully accounted for. Missing luggage you can deal with; missing people is an entirely different matter. There was one guy who made it just in the nick of time, his ride pulling up in front at 8:55. He had no choice but to go into the morning meeting wearing the same clothes he had on last night and smelling pretty raunchy. He got a much-deserved ribbing from his peers. It doesn't hurt for them to get a reminder from their colleagues that this is a business event and not a pleasure trip, even if their own behavior has not been exemplary.

Today is basically a repeat of yesterday: a full day of meetings, coffee breaks, lunch and then off to the hospitality suite for a few drinks before heading out for the night. Dinner tonight will be their awards presentation, which is being held off-property in an upscale setting. Traditionally, their awards dinner has been held on the last night but they have something special planned for tomorrow as a surprise, and the corporate execs wanted to have their stay end with fun not formality this time around.

Tonight's restaurant had been chosen before the corporate execs knew that it would be an all-male group that would qualify. The company heads loved the setting and didn't want to change it when the group demographics were known. Their private room was in a courtyard built around a gorgeous swimming pool and everything was pink on pink. The entire area was filled with tropical plants and flowers, with a white baby grand off in one corner. The atmosphere was pretty, pink and feminine enough to extinguish a cigar. After the first night, with the guys wanting to reunite the mermaid with the ocean, and last night's swimming pool escapades, the thought of this group around more water was not calming. Visions of waiters or participants themselves taking a dip in the pool are running through our heads.

After cocktails, dinner, drinks, dessert and awards the guys will be free to return to the resort or stay in town and catch one of the private shuttles and return at their leisure. It's a safe good bet that after a day of sitting in meetings and through dinner and speeches, these guys will be staying to play.

■   ■   ■

Dinner and the awards went without a hitch. There was good-natured back-and-forth between the guys but that was pretty much it. Either they were still tired from last night or saving their energy for something good tonight. With all the whispering going on I suspected we would be in for quite a night. This good behavior was just for show, of that we were pretty certain, having been there and experienced the like many times before.

Once again, no one chose to return home early and after their event was over, we bid them goodnight. It was time for us to grab dinner. I had made reservations for us at a new restaurant on their upstairs patio. We would be out of sight but still close by if any of the staff assigned to wait with the return shuttles needed us.

It was the first time since the group arrived that we were able to sit together and relax for the moment. This was also the perfect opportunity for us to review what still needed to be done before tomorrow. In order to keep the element of surprise, setup can't begin until early morning and everyone has a part to play in its success.

But alas, so much for out of sight. Apparently from down below we were visible. The guys en route to another bar, obviously after a couple more drinks, had spotted Dee Dee and gathered in the street loudly chanting her name, wanting her to come down and play with them. Laughingly she shook her head no and said she would see them in the morning. They finally moved on and we finished our dinner and headed back to the hotel to see what awaited us.

Nothing out of the ordinary upon our return. It was still early but we all decided it would be a good idea to retire in case we were called out again in the middle of the night. Everything that could be done for tomorrow was in place and we would be ready to roll first thing in the morning.

■   ■   ■

It's 2:00 a.m. and I'm wide awake. I just called down to the front manager to see how things have been going. Only a few guests had returned; the rest should be along shortly, he imagined. Call me if you need me, I advised him. Trust me, I will, he replied dryly. He and the rest of the night staff weren't too impressed with the naked pool party that had happened on their watch. Oh well, I did my part way back when, when I issued a mayhem alert. Something was up for either tonight or tomorrow. There was a definite undercurrent tonight of something being planned that wasn't on our agenda.

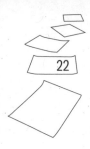

■   ■   ■

2:30 a.m. They're back. And I didn't need a call from the front desk to let me know. I was dressed, out the door and in the lobby in less than two minutes. I knew Dee Dee and the rest would soon be on my heels. Along with the other half of the hotel, too, complaining about the noise.

The guys arrived carrying bags of party supplies and other items we couldn't quite make out. Seeing us waiting for them, they tried to quiet down and maintain some sense of decorum. All they wanted, they said, was to take a late night swim and have a couple more drinks, and promised to keep the noise down. The night manager, against his better judgment, gave his OK but said that security would be overseeing their get-together and at the first noise or behavior infraction the pool would be closed.

Doing a quick headcount, I noted that Mr. Instigator and his closest allies were missing. Could the boisterous arrival have been a planned distraction maneuver? We'd have to wait and see. There was no way we could go back to bed. The guys headed to their rooms with their purchases to change into their swimsuits and—short of asking to check packages—we had no idea what was in them. Somehow souvenir shopping didn't seem likely. We soon found out.

The night manager came racing out from the back room. One of the nearby bars thought they should give the hotel a heads-up that inquiries were being made by some of the guys as to where they could rent chain saws. Apparently there were plans afoot to do some landscaping at the hotel. The guys were ticked off—actually, stronger words were used—that their party last night was cut short. The informer had no idea whether or not they were successful in their quest.

With this new information, who knew what could be in the bags and packages carried in. Shovels. Pruning shears. Gardening tools. Undaunted, unable to rent chain saws to cut the trees down around the pool that they thought afforded too much shade, they decided to transplant some of the flowering bushes around the property to give it a new look. Shovels and pruning shears, they also had reasoned, were quieter than chain saws. And they'd purchased tons of bubble bath for the pool and the Jacuzzis. After the last occurrence, we had asked that the maids prudently remove the bottles of bubble bath that had been placed in each guestroom so it would not be easily accessible on a drunken whim. So much for that plan.

Out by the pool Mr. Instigator and his buddies had shown up. Also present were several of the same ladies from last night. No idea how long they have been on the property—or if they even left last night. They could have doubled back somehow. Note to self: Check room service and other room charge bills. Dee Dee was in her element and I let her be.

The night manager warned about charges being laid if anything was damaged and he informed them that their actions could have serious consequences. They were lucky that someone had called to let the hotel know what was about to take place before any actual destruction had taken place. If they all immediately left the area, they were told, and went to their rooms, the authorities and corporate execs would not be called down to deal with this matter. With a show of false blustering bravo, Mr. Instigator told the guys to go to their rooms—this place wasn't worth wasting their landscaping talents on. The guys quickly dispersed and headed to their rooms while we escorted their female friends to the front door of the hotel. Now we're finally back in our rooms, trying to get some sleep before our early start.

DECEMBER 16

When we met up at the hospitality desk in what seemed like minutes later, Dee Dee groused that if we handle this client again, instead of a bowl of candy on the hospitality desk we should have a container filled with condoms done in the theme logo. On her way down for early setup she had seen a couple of women slipping out of rooms that she knew belonged to our guys and caught another attendee literally with his pants down, doing the deed with his "friend" in what they assumed was a secluded spot. Unfortunately, his shiny bare bottom had been made very visible by the light coming off of the decorative lamps set at ground level along the pathways. Hearing Dee Dee—she had deliberately made a sound to let them know she was there—they quickly stopped their clandestine activity, scrambled back into their clothes and said their good-byes, all the while receiving the full impact of Dee Dee's disapproving stare. But better her stare than that of the company execs, who would soon be headed down this same path.

Catching a married man carrying on in this manner, literally out in the open, without imposing consequences or at least a serious reprimand could carry company repercussions. I'm sure there's no need to remind the corporate execs of that. They know that if the man's wife were to find out what had transpired during a business meeting under their professional direction and sued for divorce, they could get tangled up in unpleasant court proceedings if it came out they had encouraged their employees to act out and provided the means to overindulge. This has happened before but not to their company, and they undoubtedly want to keep it that way. Their company image is built around family values and the media would have a field day if something like this got out. The company execs can close their eyes to the goings-on as long as they don't see it take place right in front of them, which is why they're retiring early each night. They want their guys to have fun, but as they had very clearly and often told us, they wanted to be able to claim plausible deniability.

The corporate execs want to be seen as guys embracing guyness up to the point where it will affect their company's bottom line and their jobs. They know that their company's growth isn't built by a sales force that embodies metrosexual sensibilities and embraces grande lattes, no-carb beer, facials, pedicures, chest waxing, fake-and-bake tans and designer wear. That's not who they—or their customer base—are. Their sales team likes to get down and party, drink beer, make crude jokes and sexual innuendoes, compete with one another to lead the way in bad-boy antics and one-up one another while they're away with their peers. And the corporate execs have been happy to design a program that enables said behavior if it translates into higher sales when the group returns back to the office. The couple Dee Dee's path crossed probably had assumed that no one would be up and about that early except the hotel security guard making his rounds and they could pay him no mind. No doubt there have been more trysts going on around the property, being justified as "innocent fun" while out of town. It's generally a given on these types of trips.

As Dee Dee and I chatted, other indiscretions were brought to our attention. This morning's planned activity meant that the program directors, hotel bellmen and local staff were all up and about much earlier than the guys had anticipated. Room service made surprise early morning room deliveries of continental breakfast trays with lots of hot steaming coffee in large thermos containers, fresh Florida orange juice, baskets of warm breakfast rolls and pastries, curls of creamy butter and assorted pots of peanut butter and jam to our guestrooms. Attendees were advised when they received their wake-up call that morning coffee was waiting for them outside their door. We figured that after a night of revelry it would be advisable to have food and coffee available first thing. A few bellmen received their own surprises as they encountered several amorous couples making out in the hallways with their assigned bodyguards—oops! I meant roommates—either mumble-grumble-mumble occupied, or likewise inside the room or hopefully sound asleep—and alone— unaware of what was taking place outside their guest room doors.

Guess we hadn't successfully dispatched all of the female party attendees, or they made their way back on property somehow, avoiding the now very watchful eye of the hotel night staff.

This morning everyone moved full-out to get everything in place before the guys headed down to the meeting room. More coffee, juice and muffins were set up outside the room to tide them over until breakfast was served. The meeting room was the launch point for today's event, which was a car rally created to restore their competitive juices before they headed back into the office. Teams had been carefully selected and theme polo shirts placed in their survival kits, which had been tagged with each individual's name. Until the survival kits were distributed and their shirts were put on, no one knew what team they were on. I love the element of surprise! Breakfast tables of four were set up so team members could strategize over breakfast and those who wanted to drive could fill out the appropriate car rental and insurance details and sign company waivers (as well as agree not to speed or drink and drive). We didn't want to give the guys too much time to plot together, or give away what was happening today, which is why the survival bags were not delivered to their guestrooms the night before. We also didn't want them to have the opportunity to switch team colors. They were on a specific team for a reason and we wanted to make sure that it stayed that way.

Inside their survival bags, we had packed their team shirt, matching theme logo hat, a digital camera for each of them and Polaroid's instant printer (both with the theme logo), sunscreen lotion, prepaid calling card in case of emergency, hotel telephone number, detailed road map, bottled water and various other items they would need for a fun day in the sun. The bags themselves were great. They were stitched with their company's President Club for Top Sales logo and the year, and could double as a sports bag. These would definitely be used again and again, and would serve not only as free corporate advertising but also a reminder that they had all been inducted into the prestigious President's Club last night at the awards presentation.

We had set up checkpoints with refreshments along the way so that we could track when someone went missing or if anyone ran into car trouble. Beverages and snacks would be available at some, lunch would be held at a specific restaurant and ice cream and other frozen treats would be served at other spots. The rally was based on creativity and taking photographs of specific items on their list that would guide them around our designated route. We made it very clear that speed was not a determining factor in winning the rally, warning them that points would be taken away if they checked in back at the hotel too early and detailing the penalties if they were ticketed by the law.

The meeting room exploded with enthusiasm when the guys found out that they were scheduled for a play day designed to enjoy their location to the fullest and would not be spending the day locked up in a meeting room. Talk about a burst of energy. We went over the details of the rally, and told them that a clock-in party would be happening at the hotel at 4:00 p.m. followed by volleyball, a great high-energy band for listening—not dancing to—and a beach barbecue. Found it funny that no one even mentioned the mode of transportation. Seems they thought they would be going by minivans and we sure didn't tell them otherwise. They were in for another surprise.

The local staff had been hard at work since early morning, ferrying very expensive luxury convertibles to the hotel parking lot. They had been brought down from Miami yesterday and kept out of sight so as not to give anything away. It was important that the convertibles be of the same make and year and in pristine condition. They gleamed. They were all lined up in perfect formation—great for a group photo—with the exception of one old, beat up, dirty convertible parked right in their midst, which spoiled the whole effect. That, of course, would never do! We finally determined, through the rental car agency, that the convertible belonged to a hotel guest. We woke him up to get his keys so the convertible could be moved away from ours. Guess he thought this was the place to park convertibles, never mind all the other empty spots, and judging from his parking job he too must have been out partying last night. The gentleman was not at all pleased about being woken up by the hotel staff but grudgingly allowed them to come to his room for the car keys to move it for him. I sent a continental breakfast tray up to his room as a thank-you. It was much easier than having his car physically towed out of the way as Dee Dee had proposed. If he hadn't agreed, though, that would've been our next course of action. I knew, as we all did, that this photograph would be the "money shot" that would help to get those left behind excited about attending next year and we were not about to let one beat-up convertible spoil that image.

I couldn't wait to see the looks on their faces when they walked outside and saw the convertibles gleaming in the sunshine. The company execs advised them that they would not be taking part in the day's activities as they would be having their own meeting today, but said they'd meet them back at the hospitality suite for the clock-in party and drinks. Another cheer.

After they finished all the paperwork and breakfast came to an end, we gave them ten minutes to go back to their room, drop off any pens and notepads and meet us in the lobby where we'd give them each a different route with the same checkpoints in a different order. We wanted to make sure we had everyone present before we took them outside. They were sooo excited to see what would happen next. The photographer we'd hired to take candid shots and then a group photograph was ready and waiting.

This group of macho men dissolved into little boys in a candy store when they rounded the corner and saw the top-of-the-line convertibles waiting for them. The morning had barely started and they were well on their way to having a great day.

I felt pretty certain that we'd have the rally under control. I had ensured that the hospitality desk would be staffed all day in case any calls came in for assistance. The checkpoints were in place and local staff was overseeing them. Dee Dee and I set out in our own convertible to do the advance on the restaurant for lunch to make sure all was in order when the guys started to arrive. Local staff would be meeting us there to take over and we would head back to the hotel to make sure that all was in place for the check-in party and beach barbecue party.

Dee Dee likes to drive so she slipped into the driver's seat with glee. It was such a beautiful day to be out driving around with the top down. I had, however, forgotten about Dee Dee's heavy foot on the pedal. We were lucky on the drive out to avoid a speed trap and a second one that they had positioned just down from the first in the hopes that drivers who had counted themselves lucky to have escaped the first might get caught in the second. It was a good ploy and I think the only thing that saved us was that they were both busy with other cars they had pulled over!

The scenery was great. The guys are sure to have good memories to take away from today. The checkpoints that we stopped by said that everyone was having a good time and seemed on their best behavior, which could be interpreted as "we didn't see any beer in the cars." We headed over to the restaurant and they were ready and waiting for the group to arrive, carload by carload. We had a fair amount of time to ourselves so we were able to relax, have a late breakfast and review tomorrow's departure procedures. The staff at the hospitality desk was working on bag pull lists and departure notices that would be delivered and waiting in each guestroom when the guys got back.

Heading back to the hotel, Dee Dee's heavy foot ended up in getting us pulled over. I won't be letting her live that one down any time soon. There we sat in the morning sun getting ticketed as some of our guys in the convertibles drove by on the other side of the road. Sure enough, they spotted us. They waved and called out to Dee Dee, who laughingly told them she was just showing them what would happen if they sped. I wasn't laughing.

■　　■　　■

3:30 p.m. Everything is in place for the guys' arrival back. Just like last night I'm sure we'll hear them before we see them. I am certain that the "no drinking in the car or having drinks en route" rule was violated long ago.

Huge corkboards have been set up to post each group's photos for judging. Since they're earning extra points for creativity, I'm confident that we'll be seeing some unusual photos. As far as I know everything's been going okay. We've received no calls for help or calls from the sheriff's office, which is a good sign after the attempt to rent chain saws last night, and I'm still a little on edge. I've encountered many things on-site but renting chain saws and going so far as to buy shovels and the like to rearrange the landscaping at the hotel is a first. The bubble bath and soap to put in the fountains or swimming pool . . . well, that's a "been there, handled that one before" item on the list of what to be prepared for. As for the chain saws, I had to give it to the guys. That was a new one to be added to the list.

■　　■　　■

Just as predicted the convertible car rally stimulated the guys' creative juices and the spirit of competition. One team, intent on bringing in the best photo of a specific bird's nest found in the Keys, actually rented a four-seater plane to go up in and take an aerial shot of the nest. I was amazed at the length they went to and their ingenuity. They stood alone on delivering a creative shot of that requirement. No one else topped renting a plane just to take one photograph. However, when it came to certain other required photographs, the theory that great minds think alike was proven (these are all top company performers, after all). I can't imagine what the poor girl who worked in a coin-operated laundry was telling her family about her day at work this evening. Apparently, all 50 men stopped by this one coin-operated laundry and posed nude, save a small box of soap held strategically in place. Some actually posed nude inside or half-inside the dryer, sitting on washing machines or in some other very interesting pose. And yet, we had not one complaint from the storeowner or employee and neither did the local staff manning the checkpoints. Fifty men bringing in their trousers for laundering is one thing. Fifty men dropping their trousers and running around posing in the nude is another. Man, I hope she had been forewarned. She either played along, thought it was a hoot or is still sitting there in shock. The photos escalated from there. And yes, there had been drinking involved but the drivers swore that they had not partaken. Of course, they were more than ready to make up for it now.

The rest of the night was a blast. The guys partied hard but stayed on property as far as we could tell. Night volleyball on the beach was a hit. They were out to have a good time and to win. They devoured mounds of fresh lobster, shrimp and steaks. The band was terrific and revved them up. The night staff jokingly said that they forgave all past misbehavior, but I noticed that security on the resort was more than doubled tonight. And Mr. Instigator even had his arm around the head of security before the end of the evening. They were now best buddies. The guys tore up the night but in a good way. They're finally starting to get mellow in Margaritaville and it's time to leave. Tomorrow they might be hurting and hungover, but tonight was boys' night and a time to celebrate. The corporate execs have loved every minute of it, and while they raised their eyebrows at the naked soapsuds pictures—ah yes, the guys did finally find a way to have fun with foam—I think they're very happy with the bond and the competitive camaraderie that's developed among their top sales members. They pulled me aside tonight and asked what we can do to top this next year. Right now I don't even want to think about that.

DECEMBER 17

We're standing in Miami Airport now and the scene is not pretty. Fifty grown men just realized that they are moments away from boarding their final plane home and not one of them has bought a gift for their wife or children waiting to greet them at the airport. One man, Mr. Pranked, had tears in his eyes when the thought first hit him. He was the one that actually set them all off in panic mode. Fortunately for them, Miami Airport has shopping for all age groups available, but the minutes are ticking. I see that some of the guys are returning now with arms laden, but many of the goods have "Miami" printed on them, not "Key West." Should be interesting to hear their explanations.

■　　■　　■

Unfortunately, I did end up in a position to hear the explanations. Dee Dee, the rest of the program directors and I had picked up our bags, cleared customs and were waiting outside to make sure that no one had lost their luggage. We were standing in the middle of the guys and being introduced to their family members who had come to the airport to pick them up. Tall tales were being told about day and night meetings and particularly hard to hear was how much one man had missed his wife—this was the same "gentleman" who had been having sex openly on the hotel grounds. Sadly, this was the sentiment I was hearing all around me, but I know full well that it was only hours before that they were scrambling madly around the airport in search of a gift, just remembering their loved ones for the first time in days. We were laughingly scolded by the wives and lovers for working their men too hard . . . just look at how exhausted they all seem.

That's when this job is hardest. Standing still, saying nothing, but knowing the truth. Being a master of discretion is what it is all about. But it didn't stop Dee Dee from reaching over and pretending to wipe something off of Mr. Instigator's cheek and remarking on how it looks like he left some soap behind—long pause—when he was shaving. I have to admit the startled look on his face was priceless. He looked like a kid caught with his hand in a cookie jar. Our job for this program is done. Ah yes, it is a glamorous life we lead, or so it is perceived. Well, maybe it is sometimes, but this wasn't one of the times. This was more like running a summer weekend camp where boys are encouraged to be boys. I am beat.

I'm enjoying my quiet flight home. After being away doing the pre-con and then being with a group for a number of days it will be so nice to come back home and just veg out. I crave silence—at least a couple of hours of it. I travel more than I am home and I'll admit that I still haven't gotten used to there being no turn-down service, chocolate on my pillow or room service to call when I arrive back at my place for what I call my stopover. This time I'll have just enough days between trips to check in at the office, catch up on things that need my attention and pack for my next destination. Sunny Caribbean, here I come! White sandy beaches, turquoise oceans and palm trees swaying gently . . . just another day at the office. It's the commute that's the killer. Oh well. Someone has to do it.

MEETINGS, MAYHEM AND MARGARITAVILLE: Q&A

Group Arrival

Q: Beyond having the group fly down in smaller numbers, what steps could be taken to bring a celebrating, high-energy group under control when they're traveling to the event?

A: It is always important to have staff fly down with the group as opposed to merely being on hand to check them in at the departure airport and then having advance staff meet them upon arrival. Staff can work with the flight crew to monitor the group. On one such flight, the pilot turned on the "return to your seat and fasten your seatbelt" sign for the duration of the trip because of "anticipated turbulence" when some individuals began opening and passing around bottles of duty-free liquor and giving the flight crew a difficult time. Things quieted down quickly and many participants, already the worse for wear with excess drinking, fell asleep to the relief of those sitting around them.

Another way would be to separate them upon arrival by not having one main motor coach pick them up and transfer them to the hotel. Having them split up into several motor coaches or using smaller minicoaches or vans gives event planning staff the opportunity to separate the main mayhem instigators from the rest of the group or from each other and stop their quest to outdo one another. With an all-male sales group, event planners can anticipate high energy and hijinks fueled by alcohol and competitive spirits. And if one individual is creating most of the disturbance, a staff member can quietly engage them by creating a reason that they need their assistance (such as with room assignment, etc.) and in that matter have them break away from the group.

Assignment

How did the Starr Productions event planning staff handle the flight, airport arrival and hotel transfer, and what further steps, if any, could have been or should have been taken for more control over group behavior? (Special note: In-depth information on airport transfers and guest arrivals is covered in *Event Planning: The Ultimate Guide*.)

Welcome Reception and Dinner

Q: What kind of an event works best for a welcome reception and dinner?

A: On arrival days, especially when air travel and time changes are involved, it is best to plan a light beginning to the group's stay. The dollars spent doing a full-out theme event would be wasted, as the participants will be travel weary. What is strategically best is to have them go to bed early and get rested and ready for their stay. Dollars spent will have the most impact and event value on the second night.

Assignment

Discuss welcome reception and dinner event elements and design a welcome food and beverage menu, room layout, serving/presentation style, and entertainment and decor options that will work strategically to meet the event's objective of getting guests mixing and mingling. Explain the reasons why your chosen design will work (e.g., a sit-down dinner with food stations to get people standing in line and talking to one another, or ice-breaking food stations such as a custom sushi bar, both of which have an educational and entertainment value to stimulate conversation). (Special note: In-depth information
continued

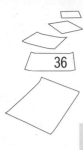

on strategic event design and strategic room layout is covered in *The Business of Event Planning*.)

Welcome Reception Refreshments

Q: What type of food and beverage should be served at welcome receptions?

A: As with any reception involving alcohol, it is always advisable to choose foods that are high in protein, such as meat and cheese, and to avoid offering too many dry snacks that are heavy on the salt as that only encourages more drinking. You want guests to have a great time but not to be rendered incapacitated for the rest of the day and evening. You can limit the welcome reception to an hour if you have a group arrival (or close it down and have the food and beverage refreshed to meet staggered group arrivals throughout the day) while private check-in is going on, and then leave the guests at leisure for the balance of the afternoon to relax, unpack, settle in and explore their new surroundings or simply take a nap.

You do not want to spend too much of your budget on an event element that is simply meant to be a warm and welcoming touch. If the restaurant has stopped serving at time of arrival, ensure the group has had the opportunity to get some food en route, especially if the group already has been drinking, Remember that the purpose is to make group check-in relaxing and enjoyable but not a main event.

Assignment

Plan a sample welcome reception food and beverage menu that is appealing after a long travel day, features local cuisine and beverages from the selected destination, is well balanced and designed to serve as a replacement meal and to act as an alcohol buffer, and is easy to eat standing up in a private check-in area. Focus on avoiding cutlery, messy sauces and large pieces of food. If possible, obtain a hotel's food and beverage menu as well as a local restaurant's to use as reference guides, remembering that it is possible to create custom menus. For example, a hotel in Tucson created cactus cookies for a dessert option at one welcome reception. (Special note: In-depth information on food and beverage is covered in *Event Planning: The Ultimate Guide*.)

Guestroom Assignment

Q: How is guestroom assignment best done?

A: When you are booking group space at a resort you will be given the opportunity to block and negotiate rates in several different categories. Traditionally, the less expensive way is to block run-of-the-house rooms, but for an incentive group that is not advisable as there will be a visible difference between rooms that could be allocated to you (e.g., some members of the group may end up with their desired ocean-, mountain- or city-view rooms, while the rest of the group ends up overlooking the parking lot; the room amenities can vary greatly as well with regard to room size and room inclusions). For an incentive program, it is imperative that all rooms be equal unless specific upgrades are requested for top performers who have earned a suite, etc. through their sales efforts. Participants will check out other guestrooms and compare what they were assigned to what others received, and if there is a great disparity, you can expect a flood of room request changes to start coming in.

For non-incentive groups, the recommended course of action is to block one room category for all, with the request for room category upgrades contractually negotiated as well as any suites for top VIPs, staff room rates, comp rooms, etc. In the contract and in your function sheets it must clearly state that the hotel cannot upgrade any rooms at their discretion without the approval of the event planner and their client. If for unforeseen reasons an upgrade has to take place at check-in, it is better to choose who the upgraded room is to go to as opposed to leaving it to chance. With one incentive group, the client made the decision to keep all of their rooms the same and give the upgraded room to an event planning staff member rather than run the risk of having any of their employees' sales egos out of alignment.

With event planning staff rooms, budget permitting, it is always better to assign single rooms so that staff can be properly rested and not be woken up with early morning preparations by a roommate who may be working the pre-breakfast shift or coming home in the early morning hours after working the evening's event. Having a single room also gives event planning staff the opportunity to escape being in a group setting and get some much needed quiet time during their off-duty hours to nap, work out in their room or just simply relax and enjoy a room service meal without people from the group around so that they can return to the job refreshed and ready to go.

Assignment

Investigate a sampling of the different types of room categories available at hotels and resorts and note the differences in room location, room size and room amenities. Discuss the advantages of each. Remember that rates shown are not group rates, which are negotiated based on group size, room count, food and beverage and space requirements, but will serve as a starting point for comparison. Pull up a selected hotel or resort on-line (the actual hotel or resort website— not the master chain reservation website) or obtain a hotel's full presentation kit. (Special note: In-depth information on accommodation is covered in *Event Planning: The Ultimate Guide.*)

Group Breakfast

Q: What is the best way to handle group breakfasts?

A: Group breakfasts can be handled several ways and you can either use one way for the duration of the stay or mix them up as a fit for the day's event. You want to create movement and energy in all of your event elements. For example, if you have a group holding intensive meetings in a ballroom, you may want to consider arranging through the hotel or facility to have participants dine in the facility's restaurant and have the charges for breakfast posted to the master account for the group. This way the attendees would have breathing room from feeling herded as a group from breakfast to a meeting room, to lunch, to an afternoon meeting and then to dinner as a group on- or off-property. If guests spend most of their day in a function room setting, they'll be left feeling as though they experienced too much group bonding time.

Group breakfasts can be held in a private setting both on-property and off-property (e.g., a cookout desert breakfast on a ranch in Texas, for example). They can take place in a private function room such as a ballroom, a garden courtyard closed exclusively for the group or other outdoor location that provides a touch more ambiance than a ballroom or a restaurant

that may be closed to the public during the day (offering only dinner service), etc.

You can also arrange for breakfast to be enjoyed at their leisure by making preparations to have the participants eat breakfast in one of the hotel's restaurants, with open or private seating arranged for the group. You can either order off the menu or take part in the hotel's buffet (if applicable), and have all charges go to the group's master account. Or, you could allow room service breakfast to be included and posted to the master account.

With breakfast, there is more flexibility and you can give the group a bit more freedom. You can accommodate the early risers and those who like to work out before having breakfast. With group lunches and dinners you need more time control; consequently, those meals work better in a private setting, unless you are doing a group meal as an evening dine-around program or privately taking over a section in an off-property restaurant or venue for the group.

There are other factors to consider when looking at how to stage meal functions and what style of seating would work best where and when. Table seating can be strategically and creatively arranged to help companies meet both internal and external company objectives. Remember that the corporate client may wish to have specific people spending quality time together for a variety of reasons.

Assignment

Using a selected hotel or resort's function space, hotel blueprint and facilities (found in hotel group presentation kits or on-line under groups and meetings), discuss various breakfast options for different size groups and which would work best when and why.

Fictitious Meeting Space Request

Q: What is the best procedure to follow if a client asks you to book a fictitious meeting for tax purposes?

A: That is a matter that needs to be discussed with company owners and your company's legal department. The hotel or venue will do as they are requested and paid for, as they will not know in advance that no meeting will take place, but if the event planning company is a knowing party to deception they put themselves and their company professionally and personally at legal risk. Event planning companies have been called in to testify when company heads have been taken to court for mishandling or misusing company funds.

Assignment

Read on-line newspaper accounts and allegations tied to Tyco ex-CEO Dennis Kozlowski and to Conrad Black and Livent (who are being charged with having duplicate sets of financial books and asking suppliers to submit invoices that would allow them to move expenses from one year to another to enhance the bottom line, with company principals maintaining that they were not informed of such practices). Discuss possible company policies, procedures and protocol in handling unethical event planning requests—financial, moral and otherwise. (Special note: Examples of other unethical event planning requests and how to handle them can be found in *Event Planning Ethics and Etiquette*.)

Social Host Legal Responsibility

Q: What can be done when guests go wild, or how can you stop them before anything disreputable happens?

A: As with any event, you do what you can to ensure guest security and safety. There are times when you will be required to step in and protect guests personally, physically and professionally from hurting more than their own reputation, but you need to know from a legal standpoint where, when and how to do it without compromising yourself and your company and your client and their company.

It is imperative to remember the role that you are paid to play. You are not there to baby-sit them, to police them or to be their newest BFF (best friend forever), as was the case where one event planning sales rep decided to join his client's participants in a rowdy naked pool party instead of trying to get the situation—with the help of hotel security—under control. The sales rep lost future business with that client for letting himself become a part of the group instead of being the professional paid to run the group event and be responsible for ensuring that everything possible was being done to show social host responsibility and ensure that no guests came to harm. You can discreetly bring in bartenders to manage a hospitality suite so it doesn't become a free-for-all. This legal safeguard retains control of how heavily drinks are being poured and makes sure that no one becomes too intoxicated.

It is important to know where to draw the line in order to adhere to your company's legal requirements and to discuss with your client in advance what measures, from their company's legal perspective, they will need on-site event planning staff to take. For example, your client may request that a senior staff member of their company be notified immediately of any unlawful incidents, destruction of property, or injury.

Assignment

Throughout the chapter there are instances of guest behavior gone wild that could have had legal, safety and security ramifications for the individual, their company, the event planning company and even their suppliers (e.g., if drinking had been permitted at the convertible car rally lunch stop instead of being scheduled for the clock-in party back at the resort). Discuss the various event planning ABC measures that were put into place, what was done, what worked and what didn't, as well as other preventive solutions that in event hindsight (usually identified in a post-event debriefing) might have been more successful. For example, perhaps a resort that was not as isolated, or a different high-energy destination such as Las Vegas, would have been a better location choice for an all-male sales group. There, they could have blown off steam in a more contained environment at night with more activities—gaming, entertainment and sports—to burn up their energy. (Special note: *The Special Events Advisor: A Business and Legal Guide for Event Professionals* [Wiley] by David Sorin JD, CSEP, an attorney and consultant to companies in the special events industry, has a chapter on event planning legal issues.)

Awards Dinners

Q: What would be a reason for moving an awards dinner from the final night to the middle of the event program?

A: For out-of-state, -province and -country events, the final day is usually spent packing, trying to fit in last-minute shopping and doing final event wrap-up preparation. Return transfers can start quite early, depending on airline and security check-in procedures, and you will find that some guests tend to leave the final event early in order to finish their personal packing and retire to bed in order to be well rested for the travel day ahead. If an awards evening has so many components that it will take hours to get through and go on quite late, it is better to schedule this event mid-program, and then do a fun or formal farewell that will leave the group on a high note—revved up and motivated for their return to the office and already anticipating what they need to do to take part in next year's company event—but still end at a reasonable time and allow guests to slip out after dinner, entertainment and final words at a time that suits them. If the farewell reception and dinner is not taking place at the hotel they are staying in, arrange shuttle return transportation.

Assignment

Compare and contrast the event design elements and event timing of an awards reception and dinner with those of a fun or formal farewell in order to gain a sense of event timing and logistical requirements as well as event/show flow.

Car Rallies

Q: When designing a car rally, what are some the important areas that must be covered?

A: As with any event element you are designing, it is important to walk through the event in your mind from beginning till end to visualize event timing and logistics and the strategic design employed to evoke a specific emotion in order to meet an event objective—as well as all that must be put in place from a legal standpoint. You need to have that vision clearly in your mind before you start to design your road rally with your destination management company (DMC). It is vitally important that it be stressed to the DMC, your client and their participants that creativity (through rally design, picture captures, items gathered, questions answered, etc.) not speed is how the winner will be determined, and that points will be deducted for speeding and for drinking prior to the clock-in party.

You must take into consideration these elements:

- How many people will there be per car, minivan, minicoach, etc.?
- How many cars will be required for participants and for staff for advance and chase cars?
- What type of cars or vehicles will be required for the rally?
- What costs are involved (gas; insurance; air conditioning; car detailing; car cleaning post rally; rally inclusions such as maps, GPS system, rally kits, team shirts, cameras, etc.)?
- How will the cars be ferried to the departure point and what costs are involved?
- What is parking access like at the rally's departure point, checkpoints and clock-in destination?
- How will you select designated drivers and what documentation will they need to provide (e.g., valid driver's license, insurance, etc.) if the rally is self-drive?
- Do you have backup drivers in case there are not enough self-drive volunteers?
- How will you determine teams?
- Will any special driver's licenses or permits be required?
- What legal documents will the drivers be required to sign?
- What legal waivers will all the participants be required to sign?
- How many checkpoints do you envision and where?
- What type of refreshments do you want available at each checkpoint?
- Where will lunch be held—en route or at the final clock-in checkpoint?
- Will group transportation be required to take participants back to their hotel if the final clock-in checkpoint is not on-property?
- What type of clock-in party do you envision that is the best fit for the event and the theme?

- How will the cars be ferried to the departure point and what costs are involved?
- Will the rally involve questions tied to the client's company and serve as an educational meeting component?
- How much time will be required to calculate the winning team?
- When will the rally awards ceremony take place?
- What will be the winning categories and prizes?

Assignment

Design a road rally to take place in your area. What would be the theme and the route? Where would you have the participants stop for breaks? There has to be something of value—education, enlightenment or entertainment—tied in to the checkpoint stops, the rally questions, the theme or the destination. For example, for a road rally in the Caribbean, participants checked in at one of the most scenic stops on the island. It was a great photo opportunity to create a lasting memory. An ice cream sundae bar featuring local flavors was set up there, putting forth a playful competitive energy. In another destination, a specific plant used in one pharmaceutical company's newest product had to be found and photographed at one checkpoint, For a clock-in party, what type of clock-in event would you create and where would you hold it?

Money Shots

Q: What are "money shots"?

A: A money shot, in event planning, is the photograph or shot in a video that captures a meaningful, memorable or magical group memory or moment. It is the shot that will be passed around the office, set up on desks, used as a company internal and external marketing tool, posted on websites and even appear in local newspapers or industry publications. Money shots are carefully crafted and created but can take place naturally as well. It is important to always have a camera in case such a moment appears and there is no official photographer or videographer around.

Money shots are used to create desire (to be a part of next year's event), or to celebrate group achievement. One company who has a year-round well-being theme that has given them a $2 million return on their $400,000-a-year event investment by reducing health and insurance costs to the company takes the top winners to a repeat destination where they climb a mountain together to celebrate their individual and group success. A shot of the group and individuals at the top would be a prime example of a money shot that could be posted on the company wall of wellness as inspiration and motivation to others to aspire to be there next year and take their place proudly in the photograph.

Assignment

Go back through the chapter and assess which group functions, budget permitting, should have an official photographer and/or videographer to capture the event elements and which should not and why.

CHAPTER

2

SUN JAMMIN'

Em and her staff fall into a delicate situation when their client's mistress—who is also his executive assistant—decides that she wants to go on the company trip. She shows up at the airport with a ticket purchased elsewhere. The situation is serious, as the client's wife and children are on the program as well. Making matters even more complex is that the client's mistress is very well known to the resort's staff, as she has made several recent site inspection trips there with the company president.

DECEMBER 19

Bliss. My time for bubbles. I'm soaking in my sunken bathtub, which took forever to fill up. I've already been down to the beach for my morning sunrise meditation, walk and yoga, and I still have time to enjoy this leisurely bath before heading to breakfast. Everything is in place already for today's group arrival and I can take a few minutes to enjoy the room amenities before the guests arrive later this afternoon.

My office checked in earlier and all's going well at check-in for the flight down. The flight is still scheduled to depart on time. They let me know that they had been in touch with Dee Dee as

well to save me the call. Dee Dee and some of the program directors overnighted near the airport in Montego Bay so they wouldn't
have to make the long trek back and forth from the airport to the
resort twice in one day. Plus, you never know what traffic delays
you can encounter along the way. It was far better for Dee Dee
and the crew to fly in, stay there and meet with ground transportation—who are based by the airport—to make sure everything was
ready on their part. In a few hours, the hotel staff will be heading
out to meet Dee Dee and the rest, fill the motor coaches with cold
beverages, snacks and icy cloths for relief from the heat, and tag
the bags for room delivery. After arriving yesterday, I had spent
some time showing the hotel staff how to prepare and package
the cloths so they wouldn't drip on the guests using them to cool
themselves down.

The maids are busy readying the guestrooms and bellmen are set
to deliver the welcome gifts to each room as soon as they're done.

All's good.

■ ·   ▩   ■

Wouldn't you know it. I was just getting dressed to head out for
the day when the telephone rang again. Oh my word. Well, that's
not *exactly* the phrase I want to use to describe my thoughts at the
moment.

My office called to say that my client has decided to bring his
mistress along on the program—in addition to his wife and children. TheMistress, a.k.a. the office executive assistant, showed up
this morning at the airport with a ticket that had been purchased
elsewhere. We had been told earlier that she was not coming.

TheMistress had been adamant about coming with the group
but CompanyPres was concerned—and rightly so, but not for the
reasons he gave her—that she should stay back and take care of
the office in his absence. But apparently she was at the airport,

ticket in hand, with a triumphant look on her face. She was booked on the same flight down as everyone else but in first class with the company heads and their traveling companions. In fact, her seat was on the aisle directly behind CompanyPres's wife. Company-Pres took my staff aside to request a suite be booked for her at the resort but in a separate wing from him and the rest of the group. To make matters worse, CompanyPres's brother, who is vice president (and I had noticed in past meetings was very hands-on with TheMistress when CompanyPres stepped out of the room), has decided at the last moment to come as well. Could this possibly be tied into TheMistress attending? He's bringing his wife and children down too. This event is turning out to be a family affair in more ways than one. The company employees who qualified for this trip have also been allowed to bring their families along as part of the incentive reward.

These new developments are a potentially explosive situation that could have us "nervousing," as some of us like to jokingly refer to it. It's not the first time we've been placed in this position—of having someone's mistress and wife attending the same event—nor will it be the last. It goes on openly at times, with the company employees well aware that one of the invitees on a program is a "special guest" of an executive. The guest may be a fellow co-worker, supplier or client whose relationship with their boss is romantic, but while the employees know what is going on, his/her wife/husband is in the dark. It goes both ways. It's not just male executives playing around these days.

The on-site behavior of the "couples" is closely watched by attendees and provides hours of discussion and speculation around the pool over drinks; other times, it's carried out with great subterfuge (at least in *their* minds) and while the company employees may not know, it's no secret to the hotel staff or the program directors. There are too many eyes and so many ways they slip up, such as signing dinner and champagne for two to the room, followed by

watching an X-rated movie. They forget that we have to sign off on every hotel charge. Silly people. We know the signs when something's not quite kosher. And yes, we can tell from the bills that we review exactly what type of movie is rented. If the company accountants only knew what they were paying for sometimes as a business expense it would really raise their blood pressure.

TheMistress had joined CompanyPres on both site inspections for this property. It was CompanyPres's way of appeasing her since she was not coming on their official company trip. CompanyPres had left explicit instructions around those "business" trips that if anyone called our office, no one was to say that he was traveling with a companion or give out any information as to what flight he'd be returning on. He wanted no surprises at the airport when he returned. The last site inspection took place just a matter of weeks ago, so this is the third time that they've been down, staying at the hotel, in less than six months.

The first site inspection was the typical one we go on with clients, where we take them on location to walk through what their guests would be experiencing and familiarize them with the resort and the location. All clients build into their program the cost of a site inspection for one or more of their company representatives. For some it is work and for others a perk, and yes, they sometimes bring their spouses or traveling partners along "to get their opinion" and yes, often the company knowingly or unknowingly picks up all the costs for the both of them. Some clients are masters of Creative Accounting 101.

The second site inspection for this particular program wasn't necessary, but it was a thinly veiled excuse for time away together that could be billed to the company and keep TheMistress happy.

CompanyPres and TheMistress booked two rooms for each visit; one was just for show and the company books. On their first stay, the housekeeping staff—concerned about what they thought could be a missing VIP guest—had reported one room being unused the first night and no luggage. Hotel security had been advised, which then got hotel management involved. I was contacted and able to put their minds at rest. As the general manager and I surmised, TheMistress was present and accounted for and happily enjoying breakfast right with CompanyPres in his suite. There was no need for concern. Their relationship had been made very clear from the moment they arrived at the airport check-in, holding hands for the first site inspection. Dee Dee had called down to forewarn me. Up until then we had thought something was going on but we weren't 100 percent sure. You get to be pretty good at reading people and relationships when you are around as many people as we are for extended periods of time.

When Dee Dee arrived at the resort with them for their first site inspection, she said that on the plane ride down they may have qualified to be the newest members of the Mile High Club. Over dinner we were treated to suggestive remarks, innuendos, sexual banter followed by giggles, and requests for bar drinks such as "Sex on the Beach," with references to the "Big Bamboo" made frequently. Dee Dee and I could barely keep our eye-rolling discreet. We bade them an early night and retired to our guestrooms to give them their desired privacy. I'm sure they were grateful.

The next day they were the talk of the resort staff. First because of the empty room and then because later that morning they could be seen making love in the ocean in full view of the hotel guests, whom I guess CompanyPres and TheMistress thought would never see them again or remember them if they did. They forgot about the hotel staff. And they forgot how unforgettable TheMistress is in a locale such as Jamaica. She is tall and willowy with natural, baby-fine, blonde hair in soft curls cascading down her back to her waist. She has big, blue eyes, wears the tiniest of thong bathing suits, has an array of revealing sundresses either dipping dangerously low in the back or plunging to her waist in the front and is very, very memorable by both her actions and her looks.

This is a resort that prides itself on their high staff-to-guest ratio and how well their staff remembers and treats repeat guests. Their staff takes great pride in being able to greet return clients by name, knowing when they last stayed at the resort and even how they liked their morning coffee. Now I am placed in the position of having the hotel quietly pass the word to employees NOT to remember this very unforgettable guest as well as the CompanyPres, and it has to be done with finesse. Actually, this really needed to be done regardless whether TheMistress had shown up or not. Last thing we want to happen is to have an employee insisting in front of CompanyPres's wife or employees that they remembered him from his last visit when he was traveling with the girl with the beautiful long, blonde hair. If his behavior had been proper while out and about at the resort and if TheMistress wasn't joining him on this trip, I could have passed off the girl with the beautiful long, blonde hair as one of my program directors who came down to assist me—I do have someone on staff that fits the bill—if an awkward moment presented itself, but not with TheMistress here now as well. I need to reach Dee Dee and give her a heads-up on who else has joined the flight and make sure that she advises the hotel staff handling the baggage that they are not to make mention of any past visits to anyone. Then I need to find the hotel general manager and discuss how best to handle this situation with his staff so that there are no slipups. We have to make sure that the message gets communicated to everyone throughout the rotating shifts and it is handled with the utmost of discretion.

■　　■　　■

The motor coaches made good time and arrived almost on schedule. It was an uneventful transfer, Dee Dee said. A Jamaican scratch band was set up at the front to welcome the guests. One man looked positively ancient but happy to be a part of the welcome festivities.

I'd made sure that, on top of their fee, they received refreshments after their performance was over and they were very happy. The children in the group were fascinated by the band musicians, who were playing homemade instruments that had been crafted from everything from car muffler pipes to an empty can. Welcome drinks and food were also served by the group registration desk but the first stop for most was the bathrooms, as the place they were to have stopped along the way wasn't open! That DOES NOT make me happy.

I caught CompanyPres mopping his brow with one of the cool cloths. I'm not sure if he was sweating because of the heat or the situation he'd gotten himself into. TheMistress was hovering a shade too close for his comfort as hotel bell staff moved in to help the VIPs with their bags and escort them to their rooms. I am sure he noted some familiar smiling faces in the crowd. I had Dee Dee step in and pull TheMistress away on the pretense of showing her the setup for this evening's welcome reception. VicePres looked like he was about to say he'd join them but I deliberately stepped in to ask his opinion about something else. CompanyPres visibly relaxed as TheMistress was moved out of sight. CompanyPres Mrs. was happily smiling, chatting with company employees and their families, and making sure that they had had something to eat and drink. She was doing an excellent job in the role of the boss's wife. Some executive wives on these trips forget that they have a job to do, and schmoozing and making the other spouses feel comfortable is a big part of that. So far, so good. Having a wife implode while on a program—especially with the kids present—won't happen under our care if we can help it.

    ■   ■   ■

Sigh. Tonight's Craft Village theme party went well. A replica of a Caribbean marketplace was set up on the beach among food stations featuring local Jamaican favorites such as jerk chicken and pork, curried goat, spicy patties, rice and peas and the like. The guests were given play money with the company logo on it to use to buy fun trinkets and they had fun bartering for the goods. A reggae band played in the background. It was a light and low-key beginning to their stay. We wanted something that would have the guests up and about, mixing and mingling and getting to know one another. The craft booths served as icebreakers and gave the attendees something to comment on. If we had just served a sit-down dinner no one would really have interacted, and on spousal programs it's important to make everyone feel comfortable as soon as possible. The kids ate earlier in the evening and were off under supervised care having their own party.

Need to talk to the hotel and TheMistress about changing her suite. She was too visible on the balcony this evening and if anyone should step outside and join her for a bit of air they would be seen easily and identified. TheMistress had declined coming to this evening's event, citing company work demands, and had asked that a hearty sampling of food and drinks be sent up to her room. Dee Dee refrained herself from asking if she would like service for two or three—she's still not convinced something isn't going on with VicePres, too. We were well aware of what "hearty" meant, especially since she was no more than a size 0 or 2 at the most. We were able to offer up a plausible excuse to CompanyPres Mrs. when she couldn't locate her husband for a period of time and intercepted him on his way back to the party to let him know the Mrs. had been looking for him.

One day down.

DECEMBER 20

Today was an all-day meeting. There were coffee breaks and lunch, but other than that they were in the meeting room most of the day. What was unusual about this meeting was that both spouses and children were encouraged to attend and they did, even with a beach beckoning. It seemed like they were grooming the kids to be their up-and-coming sales force—all the kids we spoke to said that they wanted to work for the same company when they grew up.

CompanyPres said he wanted all the shades in the meeting room drawn; he had decided that he didn't want the blue sky and palm trees swaying in the breeze to distract them from the meeting and the message at hand. At least we got him to compromise a little and let them take their coffee breaks and lunch outside in a stimulating ocean breeze and ocean view setting that would clear their minds and return them to the meeting room feeling refreshed and ready to go again.

After everyone settled in, we stayed at the back of the room for a few moments to make sure that all was fine before we left to take care of other matters. One of the other program directors was stationed outside the meeting room in case anyone needed anything. Their welcome address took us completely by surprise as everyone stood to sing their company's sales theme song, complete with accompanying hand motions. Dee Dee and I got the giggles around about the time they were singing about how they loved the company right down to their toes, and as they bent over we quickly had to leave the room! We made sure we were a safe distance away before we doubled over with laughter. Not professional, I know, but if anyone had seen it they would have admired our restraint. They were so serious about it, too! It was like watching the Stepford Sales Force in action. Even the children attending knew all the words and exactly what to do.

We swore we'd be better behaved when we went back to check in at coffee break time. That was our hope, at least. The program director outside the meeting room contacted me and asked if, when we returned, we could bring a couple of large sheets and a large bowl, which I quickly rounded up. I had no idea what they were going to be used for but I soon found out. Apparently some of the senior execs had promised to shave off their hair and mustaches if their sales team made quota and they were about to make good on

CHAPTER TWO

that bet. I left after delivering what they needed, just in case another rousing chorus of the company song was to accompany the shearing process and I took Dee Dee with me. I didn't trust either of us to be able to stifle a case of the giggles if they broke out in song again and I wanted to set a good example. Maybe there had been additional reasons CompanyPres wanted the shades drawn.

I can't believe that CompanyPres and VicePres could stand there and sing about loving their job to the bottom of their toes with a straight face. TheMistress, however, didn't have to worry about that. She was hard at "work" on her tan down on the beach. Her attire was definitely more modest than before, but not by much. She was still turning heads but the thong had been replaced by a full bikini bottom. I was just happy she was far away from the meeting room, CompanyPres, his Mrs. and his kids. Less chance for slipups that way, even though they will take place no matter how much you do to circumvent them. We've already had one or two incidents of hotel staff welcoming her back, but luckily they were out of earshot of CompanyPres Mrs. and the rest of the group. You could tell by the stricken look on the hotel staff's face that they realized what they had done but they were so schooled in their training that it was difficult for them to remember to put on a welcoming look instead of one of blank recognition.

■   ■   ■

Uh oh. TheMistress is pouting. I don't know what caused the pout but it is definitely there. Just passed her on her way back up to her room. Lunch went well and the afternoon coffee break just finished. The meeting has another hour or so to go before it breaks. I don't know what explanation was given for the company's executive assistant not attending the business meeting today, but it's better for all that she isn't found lying on the beach when the meeting breaks.

■   ■   ■

It was a beautiful, beautiful night to head out on the ocean for a sunset dinner cruise aboard a luxury yacht. Couldn't have asked for better. Everyone gathered on the dock dressed in his or her evening "casual elegance" finery. The kids had all opted to stay at the resort and have their own party. Yay for us who worked the cruise tonight and for the parents—there were no seasick mini-tummies to deal with. Hotel babysitters made sure that they were well cared for and sound asleep in their own beds when the parents arrived back at the resort. There were also program directors on hand to oversee their mini-event and to make sure that all child security and safety requirements were maintained. We—Dee Dee and I—were hard at work while skimming over sun-kissed sparkling water and enjoying the salty sea air on our faces. Make no mistake; while it was much better than being stuck in the office, it was not a pleasure cruise for any of the staff working.

TheMistress made her usual dramatic entrance, semi-dressed in her most sexy—cut to barely there—hot pink micro minidress, sashaying down the dock with her hair a mass of artfully arranged tousled curls. Guess she didn't read the memo we put out about tonight being casual elegance with comfortable flat shoes. Those four-inch Manolo Blahnik heels didn't last the night, but hey, they made for a great entrance. With legs that stretched seemingly forever, she sure got the crew's attention. She also got ours. CompanyPres had said that she wouldn't be coming tonight. Either her appearance on the dock was going to be a surprise for him or it was the end result of her earlier pouting episode today.

Who was missing in action? VicePres. His Mrs. had said he wasn't feeling up to being on a boat tonight and was worried about being seasick.

All were present and accounted for. Time to set sail so we could catch the sunset. The band was great. The appetizers and

drinks were a hit. Dinner was still to come. Couples were up dancing already. Looking back at the dock as we pulled away, I saw
VicePres hurrying down, hopeful that we were still tied up. I wonder if knowing TheMistress was onboard and not spending the
night alone at the resort had anything to do with his quick recov-
ery. We turned around and headed back to pick him up. Oh, the
games people play.

TheMistress had men lined up to dance with her as part of
their company duty. She was the only one traveling without a partner and their wives were kind enough to insist that their husbands
made sure that she had the opportunity to dance. Of course, CompanyPres and VicePres took their turns as well. TheMistress was
basking in the attention and was showing off her dance moves to
their best advantage.

Still, she behaved fairly well. There was the one moment when
TheMistress deliberately dropped something in front of Company-
Pres and provocatively bent down in front of him to pick it up,
with her breasts on fully display for everyone to see as her dress
fell open. She made a big production of trying to keep the front
together as she bent over and artfully drew everyone's eyes exactly where she wanted them in the process. And another time
when she pretended to spill some of her drink on CompanyPres's
pants and made a great show of wiping it off. She was purposely
being a tease and each time taking it a step further. CompanyPres
Mrs. was beginning to look unhappy and so were a number of the
other spouses. It was time to turn all the men's attention back to
their wives, so Dee Dee cornered TheMistress to get her opinion
on tomorrow's itinerary. This cruise was not all about her and it
was time for a work ruse. After all, that's the official reason she's
down here.

As a canopy of stars started appearing overhead, we had the
music slowed down, giving couples an opportunity to connect and
cuddle. TheMistress was now happily chatting up the crew, who

had instructions to keep her amused and out of the way. They were now teaching her how to steer the boat. CompanyPres didn't look too thrilled but there wasn't much he could say or do under the now more watchful eye of his Mrs. Their dancing—Company-Pres and TheMistress—had bordered on being very suggestive and playful. I am sure that at some level it raised a flicker of concern for the Mrs. and it was our job to see that nothing further went amiss.

Finally, we were off duty and everyone was on their own. Dee Dee and I "thoughtfully" volunteered to escort TheMistress to her room so that she would not have to make her way there on her own, since her room was away from all the others—and we did it before any of the men in the group could volunteer. If she had any late-night visitors or took a stroll on the beach after we dropped her off, it was none of our business and we wanted to keep it that way.

And now it's time for bed. Everyone had a great time. It's been a very long day.

DECEMBER 21

Alrighty then. Mild morning trauma avoided already and breakfast is barely over. Dee Dee ran into the Mrs. just finishing up enjoying the breakfast buffet with her kids. The Mrs. was fretting that it would soon be meeting time and CompanyPres hadn't shown up as yet to get something to eat. Mrs. said CompanyPres had left ages ago to run over to TheMistress's suite "for just a few minutes" to tell her about some changes he needed with regard to today's agenda. Mrs. didn't understand why he hadn't just called her from their room and given her his instructions over the phone. Mrs. and the kids had packed up a few muffins and some fruit to take to CompanyPres and were just about to head to TheMistress's suite to see if he was still there and make sure he took time to eat before the meeting started. Mrs. told Dee Dee she was always telling CompanyPres that he was working too hard, staying too late at the office and exhausted from the numerous business trips he had to take. Dee Dee murmured sympathetically and made the appropriate responses to her concerns for her husband's health.

Mrs. said she had tried calling TheMistress's room from the telephone in the restaurant but no one had answered. Had Dee Dee seen CompanyPres on her way down? Dee Dee had, in fact, seen CompanyPres when she herself was returning from visiting TheMistress's room to pick up company packets that were required for the meeting today—they had been stored in TheMistress's room while she made additions to the kits and she had not given them to the bell staff yesterday as Dee Dee had requested. CompanyPres and TheMistress were cozily ensconced, eating breakfast on the balcony. Of course, she didn't tell Mrs. that there was no need to be concerned about CompanyPres not having had time to eat breakfast *or* how the bed had that unmistakable look of a sexual romp *or* how TheMistress was in charming disarray still in her nightclothes. Had the man no sense? But I guess the last thing on his mind was a muffin run by his wife and kids.

Dee Dee said that she had dropped by TheMistress's suite and they had been hard at work—without saying at what—and CompanyPres would be heading directly to the meeting room. Using a play on words, Dee Dee spoke the truth when she said she was sure that CompanyPres would "soon come." This is a familiar Jamaican phrase that the group was using—one that expresses the Jamaican laid-back attitude to waiting and gives hope to visitors to the island. Waiting for your morning coffee? Not to worry. It would soon come. So would the taxi, etc. Soon come could mean in five minutes or five hours; it was never clearly defined. And in the language of today the words "soon come" could have a double meaning. Sometimes we're placed in the situation of walking a fuzzy line between telling the truth and telling a lie. We've come to learn that it's better to always tell the truth but in a manner that could have several different interpretations. It's up to the listener to choose what they want to hear.

Dee Dee told CompanyPres Mrs. that she would make sure that a continental breakfast refreshment tray was sent to the meeting room for CompanyPres and that it would be really helpful if Mrs. was at the meeting site to greet early morning arrivals and help Dee Dee identify them—so she could cross them off her list—as she distributed the material they would need to review before the meeting started. This was just another make-work project, as the packets only needed to be placed on each chair, but better a distraction than not. Mrs. perked up at the suggestion, happy that her husband would be looked after, and walked with Dee Dee to the meeting room chatting like they were new BFFs.

Today for us is very light. An all-day meeting, breaks, lunch and then the guests are at leisure to enjoy dinner on their own at one of the resort's restaurants. The hospitality desk will help them with dinner reservations and then that's pretty much it for the day. Tomorrow will be busier, but right now today is a welcome break. I've arranged for dinner for all of the program directors to be served in a private room. That way we can kick back and relax without the guests around and we can go over our strategy for tomorrow, as we'll all be heading in different directions. We'll still be checking in for messages and the hotel operator will be advised where to find us.

■   ■   ■

Dee Dee and I made a hasty retreat before the singing started. Apparently it's a daily opening and closing ritual. CompanyPres had received his breakfast tray, the Mrs. was happy and it was time for us to disappear and work on departure day logistics. I told the program directors that in the morning we'd be working from the restaurant overlooking the ocean—the restaurant only opened for lunch and dinner and the hotel was pleased to make it available to us in the a.m.—and then we'd be in meetings with accounting, bell staff and front office staff in the afternoon. I also gave them a time and a place to meet for dinner.

Just another day hard at work in the office. The only difference is that today my office comes with an incredible ocean view. Of course, I could have worked from my room but when you find yourself working in tropical paradise that would be unthinkable. Working from an open-air pavilion, perched over the shimmering azure water, with the sunlight filtering down through palm fronds and cooled by ocean breezes, can make even the worst program bearable.

DECEMBER 22

Busy day. Today is play day followed by an awards dinner. Private tours have been arranged for the group. The men are heading out for golfing and lunch at the clubhouse. The majority of the women have opted for the spa in the morning followed by lunch and shopping. And the kids and some of their moms are going to the waterfall, where they will have a blast climbing. TheMistress has chosen, of course, to go golfing with the men and has informed us she will then be going shopping by private car—courtesy of CompanyPres—and will return in time for this evening's festivities. Dee Dee and most of the other program directors will be advancing each of the sites. I, along with another program director, will dispatch the private minivans, making sure they are stocked with drinks and snacks, and on the ones going on the sightseeing tour, beach towels. Once the different groups get to their respective sites, the program directors will stay with them for the rest of the day.

■   ■   ■

I decided to stay back at the resort with one of the newbie program directors to take him through the steps of overseeing gala dinner preparations. After the minivans departed we headed down to the lower section of the restaurant that had been reserved for the group's dinner to see how the move in and setup of the decor was progressing. The main restaurant has two levels; the upstairs is open air and is used for hotel guests, while the bottom is more enclosed, has a set-in stage and is used for private parties—and was perfect for the awards presentation. Everything here was under control and progressing nicely. We stopped to have lunch and then headed into a meeting with the general manager to run through a few final details.

After our meeting, we were sitting in the hotel lobby, waiting for the first of the minivans to return. We still had plenty of time. I was just in the middle of explaining to the newbie the importance of always being in contact on-site and had just said the words "because you never know what can happen" when all of the sudden the hotel chef and his assistants came flying out from the kitchen screaming that their stoves were on fire! Now, hearing that the hotel's stoves are on fire when you have 150 guests expecting a lavish farewell dinner is not a good thing.

Fortunately, our newbie is a volunteer firefighter and he was up on his feet and into the kitchen in a matter of seconds with me hot on his trail, pardon the pun. Flames were leaping from the huge cooking ovens and on fire were the prime rib roasts that we'd ordered especially for this evening's event. There was nothing else that could be done except for the newbie to use the fire extinguisher on them. He quickly was able to bring the fire under control, thank goodness, but the meat was doused in chemicals.

The head chef returned to the kitchen and said, "no problem, mon"—he would just rinse the roasts off and resume cooking them. Visions of 150 guests being poisoned danced in my head and we got into a heated argument. I wanted the stoves scrubbed from top to bottom as well as anything else in the vicinity, all the roasts destroyed and new ones found, and that was simply the way it was going to be. The chef and his staff were saying no, can't be done, no problem to serve this meat.

I instructed the newbie to firmly plant his butt in the chair in the kitchen, keep his eyes on the roasts and don't let them out of his sight. I quickly ran and got the general manager and explained the situation to him. He accompanied me back to the kitchen. I asked that all the meat that had been affected be visibly marked in front of me immediately and I wanted to see them all present and accounted for after dinner had been plated and served to my guests. New roasts had to be found. I didn't care if they had to borrow them from other hotels. What mattered most was that dinner go on as planned, with no one the wiser and no one served a morsel of the meat that was sitting there. And I expected no extra charges to be on our bill. I knew they weren't happy about the additional expense, but that would be minimal compared to the loss of their reputation and the cost of being sued if they served contaminated meat knowingly to hotel guests. They saw the wisdom in what I was saying ever so nicely. Man, imagine if we hadn't been sitting there to see this take place. Timing is everything in this business.

I told the newbie he was to stay and not move from the kitchen until Dee Dee returned and took over from him. I watched as the meat was marked as being tainted and then went up to meet the first minivan, and the general manager and the chef set out to track down a replacement dinner. When CompanyPres passed by the lobby later that afternoon, he remarked that something smelled as if it had been burning. Little did he know it was his banquet dinner.

■   ■   ■

The weather changed just at the dinner hour. It teemed "liquid sunshine," as the Jamaicans are fond of saying. The hotel guests initially were not too happy that we had the bottom part of the restaurant reserved exclusively for our event, but were thankful about it when the rain started coming down in sheets and they realized how wet they'd be if they were dining upstairs. The program directors kept busy escorting our guests from the main building to the restaurant under huge umbrellas.

While the weather wasn't cooperating, everything else was right on. The food was wonderful and under the vigilant eye of Dee Dee and the newbie program director the marked prime ribs were still where we left them, waiting to be thrown out after dinner. The chef apparently was still furious at me with having to throw out "perfectly good meat." The decor was fabulous. The entertainment couldn't have been better.

I had to snicker when I caught CompanyPres and VicePres discussing the wonderful body on the lead limbo and fire-eater performer and how much they would like to get her alone to practice her act on them. They were egging each other on to go talk to her. I had seen this show many times and I knew that this talented performer was actually a man. They were in for a little surprise. Not my job to spoil the fun in this case. Mrs. was looking subdued tonight while TheMistress was busy flashing around an eye-catching piece of jewelry. She had purchased it today on her private shopping excursion and the dazzling bauble she had picked out for herself was being billed to the group's hotel master account. CompanyPres had told Dee Dee to make the arrangements. Nope, I'll happily let CompanyPres find out about the "hot" fire-eater all on his own. The man has nerve, salivating over yet another want-to-bed conquest in front of both his wife and mistress. Payback can be rather unpleasant.

But I was in for my own little surprise. Man, what were they thinking? And how did they get it through customs? These were the two thoughts uppermost in my mind when during the awards CompanyPres started to hand out Cartier watches to their top twenty-five performers, with both the men and their wives receiving one along with bonus checks in the thousands of dollars. These Cartiers retailed from between $20,000 and $30,000 each. And of course, CompanyPres announced how much they were worth. The jaws of the hotel staff, musicians and entertainers dropped, along with mine. Where had these been sitting the entire stay? The checks are no problem. It's the watches I'm concerned about. The General Manager, who was standing beside me, said that they had not been stored in the hotel safe. I decided right then that I would need to assign a couple of program directors to oversee guest bag security as they were being dropped off at the front lobby door tomorrow morning waiting to be loaded onto the motor coaches and again at the airport. Chances are, word will get around about the watches and it pays to be safe. I need to make sure no bags are left unattended because I know most of those watches will be packed, not worn through customs or declared coming back into the country, and most likely not listed on their income tax return either. Had we known in advance—and we had asked what was being brought into the country with them with regard to the meeting and awards ceremony—we could have advised customs that these items had been brought in for the event, bought in their home city and coming out of the island and they had not been purchased locally. We could have made proper arrangements regarding the shipping and handling and had them stored in the hotel's safe. It would serve someone right for not telling me about this, but it might have been a simple oversight. Regardless, I have to do my job and ensure everything's safe from here on out.

■   ■   -   ■

I just got word that the motor coach drivers have arrived. Rather than chance delays on the return back to the airport tomorrow with the motor coaches coming up from Montego Bay, I arranged to have the motor coaches and the drivers overnight at the hotel. They know they're here at the resort not to party but to enjoy dinner and make sure they're on duty early tomorrow morning. I'll get them settled in and then head back downstairs.

The men are drinking heavily tonight. They're going to pay for that tomorrow on the long, winding transfer back to the airport. Note to self: Make sure there are some sickness bags on board each motor coach. The party should soon be dying down.

■   ■   ■

I took care of the drivers and rejoined my people. The program directors and I went upstairs to sit down and finally have dinner. We had the same food as the guests did. When my plate came, remembering how mad the chef still was with me, I decided that I was better off just having soup, salad and dessert. While the roast beef looked temping, I was not that trusting of where mine had been cut from. And I wasn't up for any more surprises tonight.

DECEMBER 23

The scratch band was there to bid farewell to the group. Some of the men looked a little worse for wear and their wives were fussing at them. They wanted to continue drinking on the motor coaches and were trying to smuggle beer and other drinks onboard. We had stocked only soft drinks and juices for the return. CompanyPres was pleased how everything went.

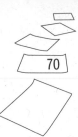

Dee Dee has advanced the bathroom stop and all is in order. She's now on her way to the airport and will arrive well before the motor coaches. The rest of the program directors are traveling with the group and I am staying behind and catching a flight to Miami tomorrow.

I'm happy to wave goodbye to the group. I'm going directly from here to another site inspection aboard a brand new luxury cruiseliner, which unfortunately will have me away from home for the holidays, but that's what happens in the event planning world. I have time for one more bubble bath and a leisurely lunch on my balcony before I finish packing and head to a resort by the airport to check it out in case it might work for a future event. Staying overnight will break up the trip and make traveling tomorrow less of a pain. Packing for both here and the cruise had been a challenge. Thank goodness for on-site laundry service. I still need to stay close to the telephone in case anything goes wrong on the way to the airport.

■ ■ ■

Dee Dee checked in from the airport. All went well except again the bathroom spot wasn't open when the motor coaches pulled in. You can advance but if you are not standing physically there, there is no way to guarantee that what you have asked for will take place. Learning lesson there. Next time I will have someone in place coming and going to make sure that we don't run into this problem again. The ground operator was supposed to have every-thing in order and it was when Dee Dee got there—what caused them to close up I don't know. Have to follow up on that later. It was very unfortunate because thanks to all the drinking, some of the men realllllllly had to use the facilities. Apparently there was a lineup of bare male bottoms taking care of business out in the open. Hope no one on board the motor coaches used that as a company photo op.

■   ■   ■

Heard again from Dee Dee after I checked into my next hotel. All
went well on the flight home. CompanyPres Mrs. and TheMistress
again were seated directly behind one another in first class, and
Dee Dee said she had to laugh at one point when they both raised
their left arm at the same time and she saw they were now sporting identical Cartier watches. And they both, unbeknownst to the
other, bought the same brand of duty-free perfume, each saying to
the stewardess "it's my husband's/boyfriend's favorite." Wonder
if his ears were burning. Have to hand it to CompanyPres—that's
one way not to have your clothes smelling like the other woman's
perfume.

At least for the next eight days, it will be just me and one client to worry about aboard one of the newest luxury liners. How
difficult a week can that be?

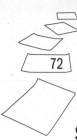

SUN JAMMIN': Q&A

Uninvited Guests

Q: What can be done in advance to prevent uninvited guests from showing up at an event and what should be done on-site when confronted by surprise arrivals?

A: In advance, the client needs to be made aware of fire marshal rules and regulations that need to be met, as well as permits that may be required to host their event elements. Room capacity falls under this area. It is important from a legal perspective and for guest safety and security that the client clearly understands that by adding last-minute guests, the guest count could exceed the maximum limit legally allowed.

It is not simply a matter of changing the table seating arrangements to ten as opposed to eight and squeezing everyone in. If you are already at maximum capacity, the room that had been carefully selected as having the right energy and ambiance for the event may no longer be an option, and the alternative choices may be too large or not the best fit in terms of layout and event design. If extra tables are added to accommodate the extra guests, then guest comfort may be compromised if the room is too crowded to maneuver around or if guests can't access food stations, the bar, etc.

There is also the cost factor to consider. Along with extra food and beverage costs, there also may be a need for additional table linen rentals, chair and chair cover rentals, centerpieces, take-home gifts, etc. There needs to be an established guest list cutoff time so that room layouts that encompass space required for tables, chairs, staging, dance floors, bars, food stations, and lighting can be finalized.

Unexpected guests can show up at local events as well as out-of-state, -province and -country events. At one head office product launch that was being held out of country, some company representatives took it upon themselves to tell a few of their local sales counterparts about their farewell event and invited them to stop by for a drink, without telling the people heading up the event at their company about their spontaneous invitation, figuring one more drink at an open bar would not be something that their company would be upset about. They did not stop to think about what would happen when local higher-ups found out that their staff, and not they, had been invited to attend the evening's festivities.

The decision not to invite the local staff had been made previously by the client because of company protocol and the increase in numbers that would mean, especially if the local guests were then encouraged to attend dinner and the show. The situation did not reveal itself until a group of 30 local sales reps and their partners showed up looking to take part in the evening's festivities and found that their names were not on the guest list. It put them—in front of their dressed-up spouses—in a very awkward position, just as it did for the company head. The decision was made to allow the guests to join the cocktail reception but not the dinner. It was explained that unfortunately, because room capacity was already at the maximum (and table seatings had been strategically set to meet event objectives) they could not stay for dinner.

All this was handled with discretion and finesse by the event planning staff, who had become aware of the situation by having a guest list and table assignment station set up at the cocktail reception. Had no controls been in place at the entrance of the cocktail party or if some of the guests were encouraged to stay for dinner and just take a seat anywhere,

the situation could have been much more embarrassing for everyone involved—and potentially for the other guests.

At another event, it was discovered when guests started showing up at the door inappropriately dressed for a private event that the lead singer from the evening's entertainment had invited potential wedding couples to come and hear her perform. The couples, understandably, were initially very upset at being turned away as they felt they had been legitimately invited, but when asked how they would feel if this same singer invited guests to *their* wedding reception and dinner without their approval they left in a better frame of mind. The event planning company gained a new awareness of what to add to the entertainment function sheets to avoid this from happening at another event.

Assignment

Using different events in this chapter, discuss various ways that integrity can be maintained both to ensure that no un-invited guests show up and that all goes as orchestrated with respect to having specific people seated at the same table, on the same team, etc., with no crafty changes being made by attendees. The guest list is just one example. Visual identification can be used, as can room gift drops tied to the event with instructions to bring the item to the event or wear the item, e.g., team shirts for a car rally, logo'd beach towels for a fun day outing, a flower delivered to each guestroom to identify which couples are going to a specific dine-around restaurant (and they will find out their evening companions when everyone meets in the lobby for departure to various different restaurants, etc.). Review ways in which uninvited guests could be handled without invited guests in the room witnessing any kind of altercation.

Flying—Two Levels of Service

Q: Is it appropriate to have some members (participants) of the group flown in economy and others (company heads and senior executives) in first class on the same plane?

A: There can be strategic reasons for having participants flown in both classes of service. For example, in an incentive program, first-class airfare is an added event element they all could qualify for and one that would be used to meet the company's objectives. You have to be careful that it does not create a negative start to the trip, as it did with one company who upon arrival had the top winners picked up in limousines while the rest were told that they were to transfer to the resort in waiting motor coaches. All of the qualifiers were winners but that is not how they felt upon arrival. Another way of doing this, putting the same message across but more subtly, is to have the first-class qualifiers fly down a day ahead of the group with the company executives and have them relaxed and waiting to greet the arriving guests at the private check-in the next day. You create the desire to be one of the top winners having one-on-one time with senior executives, while positively recognizing *all* of the winners.

   For the same reasons, it is better if company heads and senior executives do not fly in a different class from their employees, and if they want to fly first class or business class fly at a different time, on a different airline or on a different day. Many companies, for legal and insurance reasons, do have travel restrictions in place so that only "x" number of company employees or executives can fly on the same aircraft. This way, if ever there is an accident, the future of the whole company will not be in jeopardy because of losing key employees at the same time. It is important to know this in advance of suggesting a

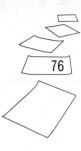

destination for out-of-town events, as you need to look at flight availability and see what the financial impact will be, e.g., some participants may have to overnight on the outbound and return or arrive in the destination early or stay a day later in order to comply with company policy regarding the maximum number of staff per flight.

Assignment

Using Jamaica as a destination, look at flight possibilities from your city for a group of 100 participants that must arrive in the destination in time for them to clear immigration, get their luggage, transfer (take into account rush hour, etc., with time of arrival and travel time from Montego Bay to Ocho Rios), check in and take part in the welcome reception and dinner (aim to have them arrive by midday), and with a company directive of only 20 employees per flight (out of the 100 participants, 10 are senior executives who want to fly first class but not on the same flights as their employees and only 5 senior executives can be on the same plane at the same time). Then do the same on the return. These additional costs, which are event must-haves, need to be factored into the initial budget at the time the proposal is prepared so that there are no cost surprises at the end. And, you will find that air availability can rule out some destinations when you need to work within company travel restrictions. This applies whether or not the group is departing from one gateway city or from across the country.

Family Events

Q: What needs to be taken into consideration when doing events that involve children?

A: Whether you're holding a stand-alone event or a series of events that take place over the course of several days or a week, such as in the case of an incentive program, when you do a program that involves children, an added level of safety, security and other event considerations come into play. In this chapter the resort selected was chosen specifically because it catered to families. There are hotel properties and cruise ships that excel in this area and have wonderful custom children's programs that can be created and run with expert help that will make sure that your event's youngest guests are kept happy, healthy, safe and secure, while providing their family members, who may need to be attending meetings or adult-only functions such as an awards dinner, etc. with peace of mind while they are involved in their event activities. Disney and Sandals resorts have kid-friendly properties and advertise "familymoons" for couples with children or couples inviting children to attend their destination wedding and be a part of their honeymoon. Royal Caribbean cruise line has a wonderful children's program for passengers traveling with children, as do many other hotels, resorts and cruise-line companies. When you are doing an event that involves children of all ages, it is important to select a destination and venue that has experience in the care, handling and special needs required to give the event planning company the extra care and specialized support needed when small children are involved.

Family incentive programs can be very rewarding to the individual and to their company. An incentive program to Disney that allowed employees to bring their children on an all-expense incentive trip produced outstanding results, but so did an incentive program to Scotland for one company whose employees were predominantly of Scottish descent. Many of these employees had not had the financial opportunity to visit Scotland and their relatives still living there. The desire to qualify was strong in order to be able to bring their families to Scotland and have them take part in a once-in-a-lifetime experience, and enjoy time at leisure exploring family roots and

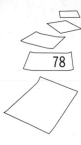

meeting with relatives. A one-day event for families was held at a theme park by a pharmaceutical company holding a meeting to introduce their new product to doctors. While the doctors met and had breakfast followed by a meeting, their families enjoyed breakfast and a private show at one of the venue's attractions. The doctors and their families were brought together for a private theme lunch and then they were free to explore the park on their own with unlimited ride and game passes. This event attracted record numbers, as did their follow-up theatre show event—tied to an enticing, in-demand children's play— that the company had secured prime opening night seating for. The same can be done for a widely anticipated children's movie premiere. For the parents, each event was designed as a wonderful balance of work and play, and to their children their parents were heroes who had created an incredible lifelong, lasting, magical memory.

Assignment

When designing an event with children involved, some areas of consideration that need to be addressed include:

- Creating pleasing children's food menus
- Food allergies such as peanuts or anything containing peanut oil, and steps taken to make sure that each child with food allergies is carefully monitored
- How children's drop-off and pickup by parents will be monitored and enforced, from a safety and security standpoint, with respect to check-in and check-out and ensuring that each child leaves only with an authorized person and no one else
- Signing of legal waivers for children's activities both on and off property

- Safety and security regarding bathroom duty
- Infant and young child care requirements, e.g., changing of diapers, bottle feeding, naps, etc.
- Security i.d., e.g., name tags, cannot be put on sweaters or other outer layers as an outer layer can be taken off, and you do not want strangers to be able to call a child by name if a children's activity is taking part in an outdoors environment, such as a theme park
- Emergency care for injuries
- How to handle separation anxiety and children crying for their parents
- How to run an adults' and a children's event successfully at the same time
- How to run a combined adult and children's event

Address each of these above areas and how they could be handled effectively so that parents' minds—as well as company executives'—will be at ease moving ahead with a family event, and design a children's theme event in Jamaica that would be child friendly and include details of all of the above, e.g., location, menu, decor, entertainment, child-related safety, security and well-being inclusions.

Master Accounts

Q: What is a master account, what goes on a master account and how and when should it be reviewed?

A: A master account is an account that is set up at the hotel for the group. Only authorized items are posted to the account. These items are spelled out in the contract with the hotel and can include

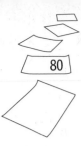
- All guestroom overnight charges (room, taxes and service charges and any other mandatory hotel charges that would apply) for both participants' rooms and event planning staff rooms
- Arrival and departure bellmen charges
- Group room delivery charges for room gifts, invitations, etc. and all applicable taxes and service charges
- All group meal room rental, food and beverage charges
- All authorized meal charges (but detailed as to what, e.g., not alcoholic drinks, etc. for lunch or dinners on own but meals to $x, soft drinks, coffee, tea, etc.) for the guests at the hotel's restaurant for any meals that are at leisure, as opposed to group functions where the company is picking up costs, e.g., breakfast for the group in one of the resort's restaurants as opposed to having a private group breakfast.
- All room charges, including incidentals (could be gift shop items, minibar charges, etc.) for specific company executives and key event planning staff (each to be named and listed in the hotel contract); incidental charges for all other guestrooms to be billed to the individual and paid for upon check-out (credit card imprint is taken at private check-in)
- All charges signed for by specific company executives and key event planning staff (each to be named and listed in the hotel contract) for expenses such as business office charges, etc.

You can check master account postings on-site each night—assign one event planning staff to this duty—to catch any mistakes or resolve any questionable items or unauthorized charges as they occur, instead of leaving the charges to when you are back in the office and have received final reconciliation billing from the hotel. On the night prior to departure, when hotel bills are prepared to present to guests for their incidental room charges, have the assigned event planner review those bills as well to catch any areas that may need to be moved to the master account in order to make check-out for the participants easy, fast and stress free.

Assignment

Discuss and prepare a list of items from this chapter that could potentially be posted to the master account.

Q: How far should an event planner be required to go if she is asked by the client to be a party to deception or cover-up—such as in the case in this chapter of knowing that CompanyPres is having an affair with his executive assistant and being asked to do all possible not to let his wife and children find out that TheMistress had accompanied him to the resort several times and that the affair was ongoing while the event was taking place.

A: Company, personal and professional policy needs to be established as to what will be done, where lines are to be drawn and what is business and what is none of your or your company's business (and something you should not be a party to). In this example, the event planning staff initially had no concerns—but there should have been—when they knew that TheMistress was not scheduled to come on the trip. They had anticipated, without TheMistress being present, that any mention of a blonde accompanying the CompanyPres on previous site inspections could be brushed away as being an event planning staff member who fit the same description, but there still could have been slips of the tongue had any staff member recalled TheMistress's name, and an advance warning not to mention past visits could have been issued whether TheMistress was attending the meeting or not.

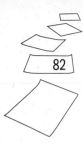

An event planner's primary function is to design an event that brings his clients a return on their investment by meeting company internal and external objectives, both present and down the road, and to successfully execute the event and not be concerned about what is going on in the resort bedrooms on site inspections and during the event. Unfortunately, though, that is not always possible, and the repercussions could be huge. For example, if CompanyPres's wife and children had seen what Dee Dee had seen—had she not intercepted them on their muffin run for CompanyPres to TheMistress's room—their marriage, their family and the event would have been impacted by the fallout.

On her own, Dee Dee made the decision to create a make-work project for CompanyPres Mrs. that would be seen as helping out with her husband's event, and, by doing so, removed possible discovery. She was not asked to do so by the event planning company. Had the children not been present at the time and on the group, she may or may not have made the same decision, and only she would have known what she had chosen to do. It is important to know and to honor and respect your personal and professional standards and to know what your company's are—and if you are being asked to do something that is not up to your standards, this may not be the company that you should be working for.

The same applies with setting company standards. There are some event planning companies that would not work in the future with a client such as this if it meant that they needed to be a party to covering up the client's indiscretions. Starr Productions did not find out what was going on until the contract had been signed and the site inspection had taken place. They thought that they had addressed the issue, and how they would play no part in what was being asked of them, when they talked to CompanyPres and had his assurance that TheMistress was not coming down on the actual program. Each event planning company sets its own boundaries. One event planning company even went so far as to hire their client's mistress as an outside freelance trip director so that she could accompany the client on his business trips under the guise of working for the event planning company in order to keep his multimillion-dollar-a-year event company business.

Assignment

Discuss how the different encounters between CompanyPres Mrs. and TheMistress could have been handled differently, and other measures that could have been employed, e.g., having the hotel in a "sold out" capacity and TheMistress having to stay at another nearby hotel, etc.

The Role of Company Executive Partners

Q: What is the role of company executive partners at events and how do event planners work with them or around them?

A: At any event, when it comes to assigning duties, it is always best to have professional event planning staff in charge. Some companies try to save dollars by using their employees or include employees that may not have been able to take part in an event otherwise to do certain jobs. but they are best doing work that pertains to their company and under their company's direction, e.g., preparing and packaging meeting material, etc. The client needs to have a polished team of professionals running the event in order to achieve the results that they want. Company employees and company executives and their partners can be and will be pulled away from any assigned duties. It happens as a matter of course, and all of a sudden what needs to be done

has no one to do it or manage it, and you cannot afford to have that happen.

Company employees, company executives and their partners can do better for their company and help them meet company objectives by being free to mingle, mix and network, and bring any areas of concern to the attention of event planning staff to handle. One executive's wife, known for her warmth and lively personality, brought a million-dollar account to her husband's business by spending quality time with another company own- er's wife who was on their event. Had she been assigned to specific duties she would not have had the luxury of time to go shopping and to the spa with their new client's wife and make her feel comfortable on her first incentive trip. She performed perfectly the role that was right for her and did it profession- ally, and was an asset to her husband's business, allowing the event planning staff to do their jobs perfectly as well. Another company executive's husband, a master of golf, was able to step in and be a desired golf partner to his wife's clients who were on the trip.

Assignment

Going back through this chapter, look at areas where corpo- rate executive partners could play various roles that would be a fit for them.

Company Meetings

Q: Is it appropriate to have event planning staff and their suppliers stationed in the room during their client's meeting or should the meeting be closed to only company employees?

A: Having staff in a meeting room is essential so that they can over- see what is going on, judge the timing, adjust any event logistical matters that may be affected if a meeting is running fast or slow (such as the timing of lunch) and handle any technical glitches or emergencies that may occur—from audiovisual to room temperature to personal illness. Depending on what else is going on in the room, it may be necessary to have suppliers or fire marshals (if special effects are being used onstage) in the room as well. It's important that walkie-talkies, cell phones. etc. carried by event planning staff are turned off or set to vibrate when the meeting is in progress and that a staff member is assigned to slip quietly into a room to get an individual if required.

What goes on in the room should not be discussed outside of the room with regard to company figures and information, and supplier staff may be required to sign confidentiality agreements. Companies have read in the newspapers, for example, how catering or other event-related staff or entertainment members have taken pictures or videos of what has taken place privately in a room at celebrity and other high-profile, exclusive events and posted them on the Web or sold them to newspapers and magazines, and are, consequently, protecting themselves.

Assignment

Discuss proper protocol, procedures, confidentiality issues and codes of conduct for event planning staff and various staff assigned to be in the room while an event is underway.

Day and Dinner Cruises

Q: Are there any special amenities to look for when choosing a boat for a day or dinner cruise that will make one boat a better fit than another?

A: Just like a room or venue, boats come with room capacities and room or venue "energy," and different layouts work better than others, depending on what your event inclusions will be. It is

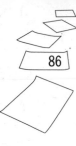

important to know what will be included and how your event will unfold before you submit your request for a quote or do a site inspection. Areas of consideration include

- Maximum capacity
- Handicap access
- Valid permits and safety inspection reports
- Indoor seating capacity in case of inclement weather or guests in need of shade
- Outdoor seating capacity
- Bathroom facilities, including easy access, cleanliness, etc.
- Cooking area (check to see cleanliness here as well)
- Bar areas (check to see cleanliness here as well)
- Dancing area (if applicable)
- Stage or designated area for entertainment (protection for electrical equipment and band members in case of a storm, etc.)
- Sound system
- Available power
- Power outlet locations
- Air conditioning (see if extra charges will apply)
- Areas of congestion that will cause lineups, etc. (to bathroom, to food, to bar, etc.)
- Condition of table linens, dishware, glasses, cutlery, tables, chairs, etc. (rentals may be required)
- Suggested menus
- Clean dock area with easy access to the boat for embarkation and disembarkation, parking for transportation (if required) or ability to pick up and drop off guests at hotel dock if applicable
- Safety record
- Insurance
- Liquor license
- Required permits or other paperwork

- Guest safety and security provisions (such as the required number of life jackets)
- Emergency backup plans in case the boat is unable to continue its journey because of mechanical problems

Assignment

Design a theme cruise reception and dinner and beverage menu to fit this chapter's event and location, and map out on a grid or critical path the event flow timing and logistics. (Special note: Grids and critical paths are covered in depth in *Event Planning: The Ultimate Guide*, *The Business of Event Planning* and *Time Management for Event Planners*.)

Shipping Meeting Goods In and Out of Country

Q: What needs to be done to properly bring meeting materials and goods in and out of a country?

A: Each country has different rules and regulations. Both the hotel that is hosting the event and your local destination management companies can advise you what is required from a legal perspective for temporary importation of conference materials (not including consumables) and consumables (goods that will be used in the country and not coming back out, e.g., custom suntan lotion bottles brought in as part of a room gift delivery), if duties and excise taxes apply, and proper procedures to follow to make sure that everything clears customs in time for your event to start. Your local DMC will help you to facilitate this process. Temporary importation of program materials will require a letter done on company letterhead be sent to your local DMC or broker that contains some of the following information:

- Quantity of each item being shipped
- Description of each item
- Value of each item (not less than the insured value of the item)
- Total value of items
- Total value of shipment

Assignment

Using the watches as an example of temporary importation goods that were coming in and out of a country and tied to the meeting, find out what would have been required to bring these items in and out of Jamaica (or another country of your choice) and back into the United States. Think of alternative ideas that may have been equally as effective as presenting the actual watch to the recipient at the event but would have avoided bringing the watches and creating problems at customs entering the country, exiting the country and clearing customs when returning home. For example, could beautifully designed vouchers showcasing the watch been presented at the event, with winning participants being told that at that very moment their watches were being personally engraved and would be waiting for them back in the office?

Surprises

Q: What is the best method to deal with surprises when an event is taking place?

A: It's very important that participants never be privy to important conversations. On the surface all must appear smooth, with any of the behind-the-scenes actions taking place quietly and quickly without arousing attention or alarm. It is important to have such discussions—and any discussions about the group or the event—out of hearing range, and that includes during staff meetings held over lunch in a hotel restaurant, as you never know who is listening in to your conversations. For example, one airline representative who had taken members of an event planning company out for coffee was discussing how they could achieve override commissions. The general manager for the mall happened to be sitting within listening distance and her ears perked up at the mention of override commissions. The mall was paid a percentage of rent based on the travel agency's sales, but she had never known about override commissions, so they had never been a part of the rent equation. Because of that overheard conversation, override commissions were included from that day on and not only at that mall but at all the malls the general manager's mall was affiliated with that had travel agency rental tenants.

Assignment

Discuss various ways staff could have handled the three major surprises that took place in this chapter (TheMistress showing up at the airport with a ticket, the meat catching fire, and the watches showing up at the final awards night) right when the surprises occurred. Also, the next courses of required action and what the event planner needs to address back in the event planning office and post event recap with the client.

CHAPTER

3

YOU WANT ME TO TRY ALLIGATOR, RATTLE-SNAKE AND WHAT???

Em experiences the difficulties of managing a client's demanding wants and whims during a site inspection and finds herself in a sticky situation.

DECEMBER 24

When I travel for business and pleasure, I'm lucky enough to be totally spoiled. I am first to admit that I love it and that I get to call it work. I love arriving at my destination, disembarking and knowing—no matter if the plane is late or early—that I'll have someone standing at the baggage claim area holding up a sign with my name on it, ready to deal with my luggage and get me settled into their waiting limousine. And it truly is work. It is often the first "test," if you will, of the local ground operator and the level of service they will be providing to your clients and their guests when the program runs. If they are not standing there showing they have been carefully monitoring my flight arrival, impeccably dressed, carrying a professional-looking sign, being attentive to my needs and treating me with proper correctness, warning bells start to go off in my head. What could go wrong when the group is actually traveling?

CHAPTER THREE

This time I was warmly greeted by Wills's familiar smiling face. I specifically had requested Wills for my pre-boarding stay in Miami with my client as he'd impressed me when we'd worked together in Key West a few months ago. I'll be dealing with a first-time client and I want to have someone by my side that I know to be good at making things happen.

After welcome hugs and air kisses were exchanged, my luggage handed over to the limousine driver to deal with, and a moment taken to freshen up, Wills and I were ready to go meet my client and his wife, whom I had never met before but who was to be my traveling companion for the next week. My client, a very quiet and laid-back man in his 60s from the deep south who had just hit it rich, was flying in with his company executives to do business in Palm Beach and would be leaving his wife in our hands at the airport. He jokingly had told me when we last spoke that his missus was a handful and said to make sure that I packed my running shoes. When I queried him as to why, he just chuckled and remarked that I would soon find out.

And that we did. Upon entering the chosen bar for our "official" wife handover, I quickly spotted my client and Wills and I made our way to him and his fellow executives and made the introduction rounds of everyone gathered there except the missus. "Ah, here comes the little woman," exclaimed my client, and Wills and I turned to see the crowds parting to reveal—blink blink—a woman who rivaled Dolly Parton in . . . ahem, how to word this nicely . . . stature, style of dress, and long, blonde hair at its most bouffant. Absolutely teetering towards us on heels that were threatening to be her undoing, the missus was just a tiny bit tipsy and literally dripping in diamonds. Whoever said you can't have enough of a good thing had never met the missus. Only thing missing was a tiara, and I'm willing to wager that the missus has one of those—if not several—stashed away somewhere.

Seeing the missus and seeing diamonds, not dainty, demure diamonds but many, many carat rivers of diamonds reflecting their brilliance everywhere, made me think of Daniela, our office manager. A hard-core fashionista ex European haute couture model from Italy, Daniela happily spends all of her off time on international programs shopping and lovingly bossing and mothering us while working. All of us in the office have at one time or another been subjected to our own personal fashion dos and don'ts, delivered in a not-so-discreet shocked tone both on-site and back at the office. Forget to put your lipstick on and dare to wander into Daniela's line of vision and you were apt to hear, "For goodness sake, woman, put some lipstick on!" When one new employee ventured to ask Daniela if the diamond earrings she was wearing were real, those who knew Daniela best knew exactly what her response would be. Drawing herself up to her full height, which was well over six feet, she haughtily asked the newcomer, "Do *I* look like someone who would wear *fake jewelry*?" Then she softened her delivery with a wink.

Taking in the walking vision before me of every fashion don't imaginable, I could just imagine Daniela's reaction when the missus first comes to visit our office or they meet on-site. But on the plus side, Daniela would finally have someone she could talk designers with, as the missus was a walking billboard. And there was no question that those diamonds were real. The missus had hundreds of thousands of dollars worth of gems stuffed casually in her handbag. Note to self: May need to add in bodyguards when traveling with the missus if this is any indication of what is to come and this is what she deems to be appropriate flight—albeit first class—dress.

"Boys, did you miss me?" the missus asked upon her return, settling into their midst like a queen bee happily surrounded by a bevy of attractive men, attentive as any good senior executive would be to the boss's wife. Her voice surprised me, as it was husky and raw and sounded like too much whiskey and cigarettes. Very unexpectedly, her laugh came from deep inside and was more of a hearty burble. "Nouvelle riche" would have been Daniela's summation of the missus.

Introductions were made, the missus handover was officially done and Wills and I were positive that we both heard a sigh of relief from the execs and her husband as the missus said her good-byes with great fanfare and a flurry of hugs and kisses and received good luck wishes in return (for us, we were convinced). Wills and I, one of us on each side steadying the missus from a high heel teeter-totter disaster, were doing our best to persuade her to leave behind the "one more glass of champagne for the road" that was being tightly held in her hand. I couldn't help but notice that the hand was adorned with diamonds and long, garish, hot pink nails—so long that I wondered how she managed to get through the day without causing injury to herself and others. Wills's charm worked, as did a promise of more champagne waiting in the limousine, but much to our chagrin her solution to not taking it with us was to drain her glass without taking a pause, sweetly hand Wills her champagne flute to dispose of and then link arms with both of us. I cued the music to *The Wizard of Oz* inside my mind as we made our way out of the airport to our waiting transportation.

I already knew my client was right: a handful the missus would surely prove to be. I was glad that we had decided to spend a night in Miami before setting sail and was longing for a quiet night with each of us in our luxury hotel suites enjoying room service, but I knew that was probably just wishful thinking.

Part of the job on site inspections is to keep your client happy. And keeping the missus happy apparently entailed dining out and being whisked around by limousine to Miami's hottest clubs to go drinking and dancing. I am positive both Wills and I blanched at the thought. It was already quite clear that the missus liked her champagne and was never prepared to let good champagne go to waste. The missus insisted that the leftover champagne from the limousine ride be delivered to her guestroom along with her luggage and wanted to make sure that the limo would be stocked when we headed out that evening to play, which Wills assured her it would be.

Dinner tonight was at one of the hotel's finest gourmet dining rooms and I asked Wills to join us (me) for moral support and to give the missus the male attention that she was actively seeking. Champagne makes the missus feel flirty, she informed us. I knew with Wills I had no worries (I'd met his boyfriend on the Key West trip). The missus seemed to enjoy his fussing over her and it turned out that they were both champagne connoisseurs, which gave them something in common to talk about and bond with over dinner.

The missus opened the menu and let out a squeal, which raised the eyebrows of nearby diners—couples enjoying a romantic evening out—and staff alike for a second time. The first was when the missus made her grand entrance, and if this afternoon's dress was casual, tonight's was over the top. The dress the missus was wearing dipped dangerously low. Thankfully, the diamonds she was wearing—a new, dazzling display—would distract anyone should anything pop out that wasn't supposed to.

While I was quietly pondering where the day diamonds had been stashed, I was alarmed to hear "Alligator, rattlesnake, wild boar, ostrich. . . ." The missus had started excitedly reading aloud from the menu, noting that the exotic specialties the restaurant was featuring this month were ending tonight and weren't we lucky to be here in time to try them. Yup, lucky us. Before Wills and I had time to react, the missus summoned the waiter over and ordered the exotic special for all three of us, with caviar and champagne to start.

In this business you have to be game to try most anything event planning life or your clients throw at you, but to date being game and eating game or other exotic fare not of my choosing has not been required of me, nor Wills apparently from the look on his face, as visions of dining on the succulent lobster or the delectable beef the restaurant was known for were replaced by this new reality. Wills struggled to put on his "game face" (ha-ha) in the name of customer service and closed his menu with a tiny sigh before giving a smile of anticipation and reaching for his glass of excellent champagne. We could already tell it was going to be a long night.

Happily munching juicy turkey burgers and salad from room service later in my room, Wills and I kicked back and planned the next day. The missus was now officially dubbed "Diamond-Diva" after finding out in the back seat of the limo that the missus changed her diamonds to suit her whims and that her well-stuffed purse was where she kept some of her diamond stash. This fact caused great anxiety for Wills and me at the clubs as we discovered that DiamondDiva was prone to dropping her purse anywhere when a song came on that she was determined to dance to.

Wills did a great job tonight, both in stepping into and stepping up to the role of dancing partner and getting DiamondDiva in all her glittering glory whisked into the hottest clubs' VIP sections with no waiting—that's the benefit of aligning yourself with the best in the business and working with well-connected DMCs. The very least I could do was feed him before he left. We were both starving from not eating much at dinner. DiamondDiva had finished off with relish what we hadn't touched. That woman either has a cast-iron stomach or maybe the amount of champagne she consumed made the exotic fare more palatable, but Wills and I just were not up to it and merely moved our food around making it look as though we had taken a few bites. I was certain Wills, as discreet as he was, used his napkin more than once as means of disposal. I made sure to leave the waiter a healthy tip because we would be coming back to this hotel again and I didn't blame him for my night.

In this business you have to be very careful not to do anything that will lay you down for the count. You can feel ill from unfamiliar or extremely rich food or from overindulgence from too much champagne or wine, no matter how good a year or how much a client coaxes you to join them. You don't have the luxury of time on-site or on-program to rest and recover and doing your best to stay healthy is just part of our jobs. We have to be there physically and mentally to take care of our clients and their guests. So we become masters of illusion as well as discretion. In this case, I left the food-disappearing-in-the-napkin act to Wills. I, on the other hand, became very adept at drawing DiamondDiva's attention to the jewelry and outfits others in the room were wearing while I tried to be as inconspicuous as possible burying part of my meal under the accompanying side dishes. Apparently bright, shiny, expensive objects are going to be very effective at distracting DiamondDiva from whatever I want to divert her interest in, which is good to know going into the week with her on my own. Rarely do you need reinforcements on a site inspection on a cruise ship, but already I'm longing for one. I have a feeling that in the week to come I am really going to miss Wills's support in the care and handling of DiamondDiva.

To give DiamondDiva her due, on the whirlwind tour we took of the property this afternoon, she really did set out to find the best Miami had to offer for the top winners—"her kids" as she called them. Every, and I mean every, suite in the hotel that was available for a walk-through had to be carefully examined with an eye as to whom it would be perfect for. Room decor mattered. DiamondDiva declared one suite done in rose hues perfect for one guest and his wife, as she knew rose was his wife's favorite color, and another suite that received full morning sun was earmarked for another who was a sun lover.

Same applied to the upscale shopping areas. No designer store was left unvisited. Man, with the right incentive, that woman can

do amazing mileage in those high heels. Racing store to store, rack to rack, counter to counter and popping in and out of fitting rooms with the speed and agility that would do a high-performance athlete proud, she often left Wills and me in her dust as we kept busy tracking her special finds to return to after the cruise if nothing else caught her fancy.

DiamondDiva so enjoyed her run-through shopping tour of Miami, the hotel, and the top clubs and being part of the VIP scene that she had only previously read about in her beloved Page Six that she has decided to add a day to their program and have all her winners fly down a day before the cruise to relax at the hotel, shop, have dinner and enjoy the nightlife before having a private lunch and boarding the next day. Fortunately for me, that's been my intention all along as her participants will be flying in during the height of winter, and in order to avoid any flight delays or misconnections that could jeopardize their making it to the ship on time, I always recommend coming down a day ahead. Prior to today, the client (and no doubt DiamondDiva) had been adamantly opposed to that, so as tired as both Wills and I were, some good did come out of all that we'd done.

We're both satisfied that our plans are in order for tomorrow, so we called it a night. It's been a long, full day since I left Jamaica this morning. My bed is definitely beckoning.

DECEMBER 25

Mmmm . . . there is nothing like waking up after spending a night nestled in high-thread-count Egyptian cotton sheets surrounded by soft down pillows, followed by a luxurious bubble bath in an oversize tub built for two, being wrapped in a cozy robe and savoring steaming hot coffee that has been delivered to your room with the morning papers. To me, it's worth the effort of getting up a little bit earlier than I really need to when on-site so that I can fully take advantage of all the room amenities and the resort's pampering touches. It's one of the added joys we get to experience while staying in world-class hotels and resorts that are a minimum of six stars and in suites that can often range in the high hundreds if not thousands of dollars a night. Designing programs that provide nothing but the best for our clients and guests has a definite fringe benefit. But there are days on a demanding program that, as incredible as your suite may be, you only see your room briefly to shower and change and head back down to do what you have to do. And this morning, unfortunately, was one of them. It felt like my head had just touched the pillow when the wake-up call came in. Merry Christmas, the voice on the phone said.

Yesterday we toured Coral Gables from end to end, including a stop at Villa Vizcaya because DiamondDiva wanted to see if it would inspire some home decorating ideas for her newly acquired estate, as well as Bal Harbour and Coconut Grove, but passed on a visit to Sawgrass Mills Mall, whose famous factory outlets might have shopping appeal to "her kids" on the trip.

The difficulty in doing site inspections with company owners and top execs is keeping the client focused on their program and busy reviewing the event elements that will bring them a return on their investment by exceeding their guests' expectations. If they're in mini-me vacation mode—especially when it's at their company's expense, as everything is billed back to their program both during site inspections and running the actual event—and live their personal life at a multimillionaire if not billionaire level, it can be trying to bring them back down to what their attendees will enjoy doing and seeing if the company is not picking up *all* of their expenses, which does happen. Sometimes luxury spa and shopping sprees are built into programs and the charges are unexpectedly picked up, as are the food and beverage charges. But if not, whisking company sales winners away to six- and seven-star resorts can defeat the purpose and make winners come home feeling like losers.

With one company president who liked to live large but give the appearance of being one of "his people," it was a twice a year battle. His guests found the destinations and resorts that he selected to be jaw dropping, and while initially they were thrilled to be going, they wondered how they were going to be able to pick up the cost for their meals and drinks, which were not included. What happens if they get caught having to pick up a round of drinks at a place where even a soda is over $10 with taxes and gratuities factored in? They were sweating, not only about the cost of the food and drinks, but about how they were going to be able to afford to dress the part and still have money to be able to step outside the resort. Stressed to the max, many of them resorted to bringing bags with them to the breakfast buffet to load up on food, fruit and bottled water and juices to make it through to dinner, as the resorts were usually located in areas where they could not find an inexpensive fast-food alternative.

But rather than include lunch for "his people," who were blue-collar workers who could not afford a lavish lifestyle, this company pres was known to spend well over $20,000 to fly on a separate flight to avoid flying with "his people." He would fly first class to another destination to be overnighted and wined and dined in high style—making a mini-vacation out of the stopover—rather than spend an extra day at the resort or fly back first class on the same plane (which was understandable because that would not project the image of being one of his people). Flying in wasn't a problem, as while he would book himself on economy and in the same room category with his group every year and stress this fact during meetings with the company accountant, his planning team and his winners, we came to know that was just for show and soon would come the request to fly in three days earlier. Next would come the request to upgrade him and his wife to first class. And then would come the announcement that his top winner should have a luxury suite, not just an oceanfront suite, and that he himself might be better served booking the presidential suite of the resort so that he could entertain in his room. The cost of $10,000 a night and up for the presidential suite was not a problem no matter how long the stay. Lunch for the group? Not in the budget?

It was a song and dance we went through every year, and when the programs weren't producing the results they wanted—no one wanted to win and go on trips that didn't include their entire family and spend money they didn't have, placing their own family vacations at jeopardy—we finally got the green light to produce an event tailored to his target audience's needs and not his wants. We did it in a way that his people did not have to incur one moment's worry about how to get out of paying for a round of drinks or try to nonchalantly pack away enough food from the breakfast buffet to see them through the day. Sales soared through the roof. Their incentive trips were then expanded to include family members and sales went again to new heights. And yes, the first-class air and presidential suites were still in place during the trip but calculated from the very beginning and part of hotel negotiations from the get-go. Previously, the company pres had been adamant about not doing that because he didn't want the fact that he wouldn't be staying in the same room type as the rest of his group to show up on hotel contracts.

The resorts were downscaled to four and five stars to make their sales team more comfortable, and destinations were selected with an eye to what would appeal to them. For example, all-inclusive resorts and cruises, where all the meals and entertainment were included, were a hit and it was heartwarming to see the difference in the level of enjoyment. Guests could relax and joke about how it was their turn to pick up the next round of drinks, knowing that it was already paid for at the all-inclusive resorts. They loved the feeling of financial freedom; it allowed them to enjoy their time away without incurring expenses they could not personally afford. And the company pres still got his company-paid vacations, only now they were called site inspections, during which his every want and whim was indulged and no expenses were spared. And site inspections to destinations that he knew he would never be taking the group to were paid for in full—the hotels and suppliers knew there was little chance of business—with monies credited back should a group ever materialize. Accounting never raised an eye or an issue with the invoices submitted for sign-off and payment. They were too pleased with the new bottom-line results to question the changes that had taken place. This business is about dollars being spent making sense not always dollars and cents, and it can be an education process. My job is to design, deliver and use discretion.

With DiamondDiva, I sensed we could be in for the same runaround and it might prove to be a challenge balancing her very determined wants with the needs of "her kids" from a sales reward program. DiamondDiva had wanted to change this morning's agenda to add a personal Palm Beach shopping trip with a side trip to see Mar-a-Lago and stop at the Polo Club in addition to touring South Beach and deciding on the pre-sailing restaurant for the group, which all needed to be done prior to boarding our floating luxury liner before too many other passengers embarked. It would be our only chance to see the cabins we had booked and we had to move fast. Being on board to do that and finalizing the restaurant were our top two priorities today—not a shopping and sightseeing excursion to Palm Beach. Thank goodness Wills was able to appease DiamondDiva last night with a promise to personally take her there as a "post site inspection" while she was in Miami an extra week with her husband after we came back. We gently reminded her that what she was requesting today was not possible as this was Christmas Day. Stores would be closed and not likely to be amenable to opening up for her to check them out no matter how good our DMC connections. What Wills pulled off last night had been truly amazing and a sign of a very connected ground operator. We had cautioned our client in advance of the difficulties that could be encountered doing a site inspection over the holidays.

He promised her they'd do it in style, with a white limousine—we had learned her color preference for limousines—and the finest champagne chilled and ready for her. I'm happy to leave that in Wills's capable hands. I'll send down Daniela as backup, as I'll be out of country again and DiamondDiva is a two-man operation. Note to self: When the program goes out, assign Dee Dee exclusively to oversee DiamondDiva and add in more staff. I have a feeling we are going to need them. It's only the start of the first full day and I am already mentally and physically exhausted.

Time to get out of bed and meet Wills for a pre-breakfast rendezvous before meeting up with DiamondDiva and discovering what kind of diamonds go with eggs Benedict and mimosas.

JANUARY 1

Sighhhhhhh . . . This is the sound of me relaxing after an incredible week of playing baby-sitter to DiamondDiva and my second long sigh of the day. I could kiss the hotel manager where I am staying tonight for putting me up in the hotel's presidential suite. He must have taken pity on how exhausted I look and thought I needed something special to perk me up.

My client had been dead-on in saying that looking after "the missus" would have me wishing I had running shoes on. DiamondDiva had kept me on the run from early morning till the wee hours of the night with barely a moment alone to catch my breath. How can one woman talk, shop and consume that much champagne and caviar? My head is still reeling and we haven't even run our first program yet. It had been so great to see Wills waiting with our limo when we disembarked yesterday and to know that I had another body to help me get through the last of our official site inspection duties. This time when we met up with my client and his executives, it was Wills and me breathing a sigh of relief that our duty was done and we had returned "the missus" in one piece.

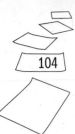

When we'd boarded the ship a week ago DiamondDiva had been positively giddy from the champagne, the excitement of going to sea for the first time, the prospect of duty-free shopping and being able to dance till dawn. I had the feeling that my client—DiamondDiva's hubby—was not much of a dancer and she was enjoying this time to let loose and have some fun while under supervised care, and I was elected to be the supervisor.

Going in with a new client I didn't know what I didn't know about their personal habits and code of conduct. Next time round I will be better prepared to tailor a site inspection to DiamondDiva's very unique requirements and bring reinforcements if possible. Normally, on a cruise site inspection it is just a matter of getting on, sailing for a couple of days with your client, familiarizing yourself with the ship and adding program enhancements that come about as a result of spending one-on-one time alone with your client and getting to know their hot buttons, then flying home from one of the ports of call after a maximum three or four nights onboard. Some cruise site inspections even take just one day and involve flying in and out and doing a quick tour of the ship, top to bottom, while it is in port. But DiamondDiva's program was different in that we were setting up special events in each port of call and that meant staying on the ship for the entire duration to show her what would be done and for me to have time to get to meet the local DMCs before I flew in the day before the actual event.

If I had to do it over again, knowing how demanding DiamondDiva is around having her personal—not program—wants, like shopping, drinking and dancing catered to, I would've set up our site inspection exactly as the actual program will run, with Dee Dee, who will be leading the program, onboard, and with me arriving in each port of call the day before our event to make sure that everything goes as planned. That way, DiamondDiva would have a playmate while I was able to focus on work. Juggling the two this past week had been trying—on both my patience and my will.

I learned it was not safe to leave DiamondDiva on her own when she was drinking, feeling flirty and hell-bent on having the time of her life. Too bad clients and their guests don't come with warning labels. It would definitely make this job easier sometimes.

Knowing some things in advance can be a saving grace and I should have found out a little more when DiamondDiva's husband made the "quite a handful" remark and mentioned the need to wear running shoes. He was just so quiet that I couldn't imagine how different his wife would be, but the combination must work as they have been married over 30 years. However, I think I now know why the mister finally put the missus in charge of all company events and gave her free rein on going on weeklong or more trips: the cost of the trip was nothing in comparison to making his wife happy, and in return the week of sweet peace it bought him while she was being well cared for was no doubt priceless.

I'll admit that I just felt a slight chill—our future site inspection trips with this client, to Mexico and Africa, just flashed into mind and each one of them is well over a week in duration.

After spending almost every minute together for more than a week, I now know to plan and prepare for future trips with DiamondDiva. I feel as though I've just run a never-ending marathon and am physically, mentally and emotionally exhausted. How does her husband do it?

I learned: That DiamondDiva does not "do" downtime. Holding center court, drinking, dining, dancing, reading fashion magazines and shopping for diamonds and designer wear are some of her personal passions. I swear that in the duty-free shops steam was coming off of her prestige black credit card with unlimited spending. I learned more this past week about the cut, color, clarity, carats and cost of diamonds than I ever intended to in my life. Who knew there were so many types of cuts of diamonds? Old cuts, fancy cuts, step cuts, mixed cuts, rose cuts—I saw them all,

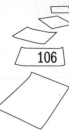

but nothing would do. DiamondDiva wanted me by her side even though I offered to set up a personal shopping trip for her so that I could tend to business. Man, I missed having Wills or Daniela with me on this trip. And then within each cut type there were different styles. Again, who knew? DiamondDiva did. And we saw them all in gold, white gold and platinum settings. I am positive that DiamondDiva left not one duty-free jewelry store unvisited. Shopping in Miami had been a breeze compared to this week's endurance test. And we had done it in style and comfort with a private limousine—white, of course—in each port of call. I was truly amazed when we walked into a designer dress shop and asked the salesperson if a particular dress was one that had been featured in "x" magazine's last issue on page (fill in the blank) and the salesperson said yes. I came to know that was not just a rare occurrence and that DiamondDiva studied those magazines with the intensity of someone studying to pass the bar.

I learned: That "I'm parched" is code for "we need to order another bottle of champagne." And one bottle of champagne in the limousine was not enough. We once had to make a champagne run in the middle of nowhere because we had run out. The limo driver found an off-the-beaten-track store that sold liquor and proudly came out clutching a dusty bottle of champagne in his hand. He had been a man on a mission and was happy when DiamondDiva quietly settled back down to enjoy her warm champagne—not stopping long enough to let it chill.

I learned: That other than seeing all the suites that had been blocked for her group and the two main dining rooms—to decide which color and decor scheme she wanted "her kids" to experience—DiamondDiva had pretty much seen all she wanted of the ship, with the exception, of course, being the champagne and caviar bar, the casino and the nightclubs, which were nightly rituals. She didn't want to see the spa, gym, nightly entertainment—unless it led to dancing—or even just sit and enjoy the view from her private balcony, which I was longing for both her and me to do, but separately. On the other hand, she did like the fact that her suite came with a bathtub. Note to self: Check out the availability of bath butlers at future site inspection resorts in the hope that the enticement of a luxury bubble bath will buy me or whoever else is on-site a moment's peace.

I learned: That even being caught in a major storm at sea—where the glass doors to outside were tied closed in some areas and the elevators were shut down for safety—would not deter DiamondDiva from wearing her Jimmy Choos.

I learned: That even though it is not in your job description, you may be required to hold back your client's hair and keep their diamonds out of harm's way when they are being sick—not from rough seas, which would be understandable for first-time cruising tummies, but from switching to drinking Don Julio 1942 tequila out of a champagne flute. The lime should have clued me in that something was different and that DiamondDiva was not just drinking champagne any longer. Or perhaps I should have paid more attention when DiamondDiva started insisting that all the men in the club call her Rosita, which in no way was a variation of her name. It was the Latin bar that did DiamondDiva in.

And sometimes you will find yourself—with a resort or cruise medical staff member brought in for assistance as a legal precaution—standing by with large plastic bags at the ready to hold the clothes your client is taking off in front of you as they prepare to step into the shower assisted by medical staff to "freshen up" after throwing up all over themselves. Thankfully I could just hand over the clothes being dropped in said bag that desperately needed cleaning after their Rosita encounter to someone else to deal with, along with a large tip.

But alas, my duties did not end there. Someone had to sit and look after the now incapacitated missus to make sure that she was alright. DiamondDiva begged me to stay and not let the crew see

her that way, and with the medical assistant's OK I finally did get to see a glorious sunrise over the incredibly turquoise blue ocean from a balcony—just not mine and not done in the soothing meditative manner I had hoped, followed by a yoga workout session. Unfortunately this sunrise was experienced with the doorway leading out to the balcony wide open to air out the room, while keeping a careful eye on DiamondDiva and the champagne bucket by the bed that was now serving another purpose. No matter how beautiful the sunrise, it's not quite the image you want to linger in your mind.

DiamondDiva's biggest concern in the morning when she recovered was hot coffee and where had she lost one of her artificial nails. She was on her own for that one and she would not consider going to the ship's beauty shop to have a manicure. She proudly told me that she always does her own hair—cut, color and 'do (and favored Texas pageant hair; that I had long ago guessed)— manicures and pedicures, and would never consider spending money on having them professionally done. We all have our little quirks. DiamondDiva would pay thousands and thousands every day on a new bauble or designer gown without blinking an eye but not a couple of hundred dollars once a month to achieve a more polished look. Maybe Daniela could take her under her very refined wing and teach DiamondDiva the value to be found in those life pleasures and how they can complement, not compete with, her other self-pampering passions. Actually, housekeeping did find the missing nail when DiamondDiva returned to her freshly made-up cabin after a hearty breakfast. Does nothing kill her appetite? She happily reported that her missing nail was placed oh so carefully in the middle of her bedroom pillow and she waggled her diamond-filled fingers in my face to show me that it was now firmly affixed again.

I learned: That DiamondDiva likes to be the center of attention and preferably in the center of a circle of men admiring all her visible assets, be that her diamonds or her double Ds. It doesn't matter which as long as they are all willing to be her partner in drinking and dancing till dawn. My job was to hold onto her purse, which was now stuffed alarmingly full of her newest acquisitions, to make sure that she made it safely back to her cabin alone, and to do nothing to distract her circle of admirers from paying homage to only her.

This lesson I learned when another event company owner, on vacation with her husband, stopped by to say hello to me, wearing a very risqué dress that featured a game of tic-tac-toe in faux diamonds across her otherwise bare back. Smoke was practically coming from DiamondDiva's ears when the men took their focus off her to play-fully attempt to play a game of tic-tac-toe on the other event company owner's back. Seeing that my client was clearly not happy with this turn of events, the other event planner gracefully took her departure, casting me an "I'm so sorry" look before she left. Not surprisingly, DiamondDiva asked me later that night to find out from my col-league who had made that dress and where she had purchased it. Visions of DiamondDiva dressed in that provocative dress—but with the tic-tac-toe done in real not faux diamonds—came instantly to mind and I knew I would very likely see her wearing that same style dress when we returned on the cruise with "her kids."

I learned: That where there is will, there is a way and you can only baby-sit your clients so far. I was startled early one morning as I opened my cabin door to go for an early run to see a man in formal dress buttoning up his shirt, bowtie in hand, step out of DiamondDiva's suite, which was just down from mine. I could hear her giggles coming from inside the room as she said her good-byes. I quickly stepped back inside my room but not before the gentleman's eyes met my shocked gaze. When we met up later for breakfast, DiamondDiva said nothing about her caller and I never asked. That is part and parcel of being a master of discretion and what she did or did not do was between her and her husband. I was just thankful that whatever took place did so discreetly.

During one event, one couple, each married to other partners, was caught having sex in one of the men's washroom stalls. Ever

since that time, I have tried to include bathroom attendants in my programs to help limit guest opportunity to embarrass themselves by doing drugs or making out in public facilities. You would be surprised how often this goes on. The coat check area, if left unattended, is another popular hideaway spot, as is behind curtains. One celebrity was discovered by event security (off-duty police officers on pay duty) in a very compromising, hot and heavy clinch with another individual and came close to being exposed to the room (and their respective partners) as the amorous couple got carried away and caught up in their alcohol-fueled lust for one another.

And I tell my clients straight out why I am recommending they include a bathroom attendant as a program enhancement. Sure, it's a nice touch to have an attendant there to hand you a towel and make sure that the room stays presentable, but know that one of their other functions is to make certain that guests stay presentable as well and that nothing takes place under their observant eyes that could cause the venue or club to lose their liquor or operating license.

I had managed to change the subject when my client laughingly asked me during our DiamondDiva handoff if his wife had been a "good girl." When DiamondDiva ordered one more glass of champagne for the road I took the opportunity to say my goodbyes. This is where I had come in. It was my turn to give a great sighhhhhhh as I walked away after promising to be in touch soon to finalize their cruise details and the other pending site inspections. Wills was waiting to meet me outside—good, good man—with the limousine that was booked to take me to my overnight hotel. Before I could totally relax, I needed to brief him on how to handle his upcoming shopping excursion with DiamondDiva and then the rest of the day was mine to check in with the office, catch up on e-mails and take time to totally pamper myself for 24 hours in this wonderful suite prior to heading home again this afternoon for a quick layover before departing to one of my favorite spots in Arizona.

YOU WANT ME TO TRY ALLIGATOR, RATTLESNAKE AND WHAT???: Q&A

Setting Client Boundaries

Q: How far should you professionally go with a client to meet their personal—not business—wants?

A: It is important to establish personal and professional boundaries and to have a clear understanding of what you will and will not do, and what, from a legal perspective, you should not do. Event planners have been asked to accompany their clients into places they would never set foot into in their real life. It is one thing to be asked to sample exotic food and another to be asked to accompany them to see a live sex show in a faraway land or set them up with a "booty call."

It is also important to establish with company lawyers how to address different issues with clients, be fully prepared in knowing where and what would cross legal and professional business and personal integrity lines, and know when support needs to be brought in to protect yourself and the company from lawsuits. For example, in this chapter, when DiamondDiva was ill from overindulging, medical assistance was called to ensure that the client was okay and they assisted in helping the client to get cleaned up. Failure to do so, had anything happened—such as the client slipping or falling while getting into or out of the shower, dying of alcohol poisoning, or choking in her sleep if she were sick again—after being left on her own would have resulted in lawsuits based on negligence. Choosing to sit by the client as she slept after medical staff had said there was no danger showed care and responsibility, but it may have been advisable to have had professional

medical staff sit with her as opposed to an event planning staff member not trained in this area. That is where it is important to know where and what to do to protect yourself, your company and your client, and to know where and when to bring backup in.

Assignment

Review the chapter and discuss areas where Em had to make judgment calls as to how to best proceed with her client's out-of-control drinking and behavior. Em might have left herself open to legal action, e.g., permitting a nonstop flow of champagne to be readily available, etc.

Selecting Hotels or Suppliers

Q: On site inspections, what other tests are there that event planners can do to see if the caliber of their chosen hotel or suppliers is up to the job?

A: Tests range from leaving a glass under a bed or in a hallway to see how quickly they are found and removed, to noting whether or not there is a welcoming message from the hotel showing awareness of your arrival. One hotel's general manager had cards printed that were placed under the beds in the suites saying, "yes, we check under here too" that I am sure gave event planners using that hotel a smile and showed the attention to detail with which this hotel was run. One event planner did a spot check on his site inspection to see a room being set up for a luncheon meeting and found water glasses being set out that still had dried pulp attached to them, and this was on top of seeing a room service cart sit for over a day, full of empty dishes and leftover food, with no staff members attending to it, although many passed by.

A site inspection is a dry run by the hotel, your DMC and other suppliers to show you how they operate and to demonstrate the level of service you will receive when you return with your group and usually takes place before the contracts are signed. If they are not up to par then, that's the time to investigate your alternatives.

Assignment

Discuss the different opportunities in this chapter that presented themselves to test the level of service of the hotel and the services provided by the DMC, such as airport arrival, limousines and the cruise ship. What would you look for that would demonstrate top-level commitment to your group?

Event Planner's Role on a Site Inspection

Q: On a site inspection, are you required to be with the client 24/7?

A: Site inspections are not meant to be a leisurely vacation or shopping trip. Instead, they are designed to be a quick review of the event, all of the event elements, venues and the destination. Generally a site inspection is done within a couple of days and the pace is intensive. You will find that you are with the client from early morning till early morning (after midnight) in order to accomplish all that you need to do in the time permitted.

A schedule should be worked out in advance with a copy of the site itinerary given to the client that shows them a clear beginning and end to the day. Identify any time at leisure— for them to enjoy the hotel's facilities, which is important for them to experience as well—that you require built in so that you can spend the time meeting with any suppliers one on one.

Dancing with the client, minding their purse and valuables while they are up dancing, and baby-sitting them when they are drunk can lead to potential problems, legal and otherwise. It is important that a business tone, not a vacation tone, be set from the very beginning and that a professional demeanor is shown. Each person and each company has different personal and professional boundaries, and you need to know where yours are and what is expected of you as your company's legal representative.

Assignment

Design a site inspection itinerary using sample ports of call aboard a cruise ship sailing out of Miami with a themed event scheduled to take place in each.

Maintaining Health and Energy

Q: How do event planners keep themselves healthy on the go?

A: They make time to eat healthy, to get rest and to have time away from the group to re-center, which is why budgeting for staff single rooms is important. You can't afford to get sick on a site inspection or during a program, as each person has a role to play. Taking care of you is equally as important as taking care of the event. If you and your staff are running on fumes instead of food that is fuel for your body and mind, not taking mental health workout breaks and not getting sleep when you can, it will show up in the program because you will not be able to bring your best to each day. Going flat out will take a toll.

One very successful freelance event planner, who travels at least 300 days of the year around the world, eats the same meal every day no matter where she is in the world, only drinks water or juices (avoids caffeine) and after her shift is done, she always takes a workout walk to have space to decompress and then gets eight hours of rest. Successful event planners do not party after hours and only take time out to shop or sightsee on their time off, after they have first taken care of their mind, body and soul. What they bring to events—their energy, their being—is in demand and that is because they are always giving their best because they have given their best to themselves.

Assignment

Go back to your site inspection itinerary and look at how much time has been factored in for self-care, e.g., meals, sleep, etc., and where more or less needs to be worked in to give better balance.

Staffing a Site Inspection

Q: How many people should be budgeted for on site inspections?

A: If possible, it is always advisable to have two people from the event planning company go so that one can advance and ensure all is ready—just as would take place on the actual program and again another test of your hotel's and suppliers' abilities. Doing so also ensures that one can have time to do follow-up when and where needed while the other is tending to the client.

Generally, for smaller programs, one client company representative is sent. At times a request will be made for it to be a senior executive and their spouse, who can offer a spouse's perspective as well, which also can be code for "mini-vacation perk." For larger programs, members of the client's event planning committee may go and there could be as many as four or more decision makers on the site inspection.

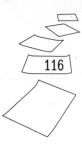

It is important that the event planning company be fully represented in order to conduct the site inspection and meet the demands of multiple clients.

Assignment

Go back to the site inspection as it is detailed in the chapter and look at where having extra event planning staff would have been an asset.

Ensuring Smooth Sailing on a Cruise Program

Q: The chapter mentions the importance of having the group arrive early for a cruise departure and overnight in Miami, budget permitting. Why is this?

A: Cruise ships will set sail at their scheduled time. If planes are delayed because of weather, guests who have missed the sailing time will have to be flown from Miami to the next port of call or the one following that, depending on flight availability and schedule, even though the ship may not reach that port for the next day or so. The same applies if any luggage goes missing. With the ship departing the same day that the participants arrive, the luggage, once tracked down, may take a couple of days to catch up with its owner.

Assignment

Design a sample pre-cruise stay in Miami. Spend only with minimum dollars as this is not the true kickoff to the client's program—that will take place aboard ship. On the sample cruise itinerary used above, look to see when a passenger or her luggage would be able to first connect with the ship.

Maximizing Return on Investment

Q: How do you direct the client with champagne tastes to choose a program designed to please their attendees and meet company objectives as opposed to fulfilling their personal wants?

A: It is important to educate the client on strategic event design and the purpose a specific event element plays in helping their company maximize meeting all of their objectives. (Special note: *The Executive Guide to Corporate Events and Business Entertaining* covers how to determine all company objectives and which style of events will best deliver them.) It is important to keep bringing them back to the investment focus of their event. There are ways to meet their personal wants as well as deliver the right event style and inclusions for the participants.

Assignment

In this chapter it was discussed how one client's personal wants were managed. Discuss other strategies that might work.

Staffing

Q: Is there a set event planning staff ratio for events that needs to be costed in?

A: Each event is different. Some companies send one event director for 25 guests, some one for 50, others one for 75, but what ultimately determines the number of staff needed for successful event execution is the event elements and inclusions and what will be required to manage all effectively in different locations.

On a cruise program where all events are taking board on ship, the number of staff required could be less than on a cruise program where something is scheduled to take place in

every port of call, as you'll require advance staff on location as well as staff onboard the cruise ship—but if the program that is taking place all onboard the ship is intensive the same number of staff may be required. You also need to have sufficient staff on hand both for land and sea programs in case of emergency situations. For example, on one cruise a participant became ill and had to be airlifted to a local hospital. An event planning staff member flew with them and their family members to make sure that they were looked after, and the balance of the event planning staff managed the rest of the program comfortably as they could still handle the workload minus one staff member. On another program, one event planner had to leave and fly home due to a sudden death in their family. You never know what can come up on program and you can't afford to jeopardize an event's success by not having adequate staffing. As you are designing your event, it will become apparent where staffing will be required and the numbers required.

Assignment

Using the advance stay in Miami and a seven-night cruise program with a special event in each port of call, work on determining the required staff members to operate the event.

The Value of a Site Inspection

Q: On a site inspection, is there anything that you can do to help build a better program that is a good fit for both the client and their attendees?

A: Attention to detail is key on site inspections, as is being attuned to what the client is saying. In this chapter it was readily apparent that DiamondDiva loved white stretch limousines. That was an easy item to note and remember to have in place for all her individual limousine needs as well as when the group was traveling by limousine. Seeing a lineup of white stretch limos waiting for "her kids" was pleasing to her and there was no extra cost involved to do so except noting it and making sure that the non-spoken request was in place. The same applied to discovering DiamondDiva's favorite brand of champagne and making sure that was the brand that was served (budget permitting) or at least in her room as a welcome gift from the event planning company.

It is important to note and take notes on each client's personal and professional preferences and build them into their events and build on them. One company president was an avid golfer and event destinations presented to him always featured desired courses that he personally wanted to play at. To have presented a location without a great course would have been a waste of time. The key was finding a destination that would be appealing to his participants and allow the company president to cross off his list playing at another dream golf course.

Assignment

Think about DiamondDiva's likes. After the cruise and their upcoming trip to another tropical location (that fed her love of tequila, dance and music) and then Morocco (which appealed to her love of the exotic), what would be a recommended destination that might have appeal to her personally and to her attendees as well, and why?

Personal and Professional Reputations

Q: Why is it important to establish company policy regarding client care and handling?

A: Personal and professional reputations are at stake. One foolish move can limit your career. For example, if DiamondDiva successfully asked Em to carry back some of her diamond purchases to aid her going through customs, the result could be a fatal career and personal move for Em. If she were caught doing something illegal, she would have that in her file forever and it could make flying into other countries difficult and work permits, if required, impossible to obtain, depending on the charges. Having a set company policy stating that event planners may only carry their own personal and business material in and out of country takes the burden off the event planner and protects them and their company.

It is also important to find out where the client stands on certain issues. Some clients want the event planning staff to eat with their participants and are offended if their offer is not accepted, but it can be graciously declined citing a need to discuss event logistics for the next day over dinner away from their guests if event planning company policy is to maintain a professional distance. Others don't want event planning staff to be included in their meal functions. In both cases the solution is to set up a separate room for staff meals close enough to monitor what is going on in the room but also give the event planning staff a chance to relax and recharge as well as discuss business without anyone privy to their conversation.

Assignment

List different areas under client care and handling where it would be important to have clear company direction and discuss why. For example, what do you do if a client has too much to drink and wants you to dance with them, or wants you *not* to dance with them or their guests?

CHAPTER

4 WEDDING DAZE

Em saves the day—or rather the cake—when attending a personal not professional event. Every personal and professional event that you do or attend provides the opportunity to learn and develop your event planning design and operations skills and take your creativity to new levels.

JANUARY 15

What a day. Attending my friend's wedding as a guest was almost as stressful as running an event. Part of the nature of the industry. Your mind never shuts off when an event is unfolding in front of you and it doesn't matter if it's your event or someone else's. There are just so many opportunities to learn what to do and what not to do, if you keep your eyes open.

I can remember when I was first starting out in the business and attending a supplier presentation at a new venue. That event was a true eye-opener of what to do and what not to do at that venue and little caring touches that would work at other events. I loved how they had people stationed in the parking lot across the street with double umbrellas to walk people from their car to the venue in case they were not prepared for the sudden thunderstorm.

And the sax player at the top of the stairs by the entranceway set the tone for the evening ahead. That was the good.

Stepping inside, the bad was very apparent. They had set up the buffet so that it was one-sided, not accessible from both sides. The waiting line was endless. They hadn't set up multiple food stations to draw people into the room and create a better room flow. Instead, they compounded the problem by stationing the buffet right by the coat check and the two lines were crossing and causing confusion and congestion. Those were great learning lessons and I had only just stepped 10 feet into the event.

And I will never forget the disastrous boat cruise I went on for another supplier event. When people arrived at the dock, the first thing they saw was garbage piled around. Then, when guests went to board, it was discovered that the gangplank was missing. Imagine the women in heels, including me, having to jump from the pier to the boat. And the learning lessons did not stop there. During the cruise, the boat's electricity went out and there was no backup generator. That disrupted the food preparation and service. When the boat finally returned to the dock, no one had done anything to resolve the problem of the missing gangplank and guests had to jump from the boat to the pier after spending time drinking, and not everyone was as surefooted exiting as they were arriving. I knew when I left that that was one boat cruise I would not be booking for my clients.

The wedding today, overall, went pretty smoothly. From an event planning perspective, the one area of concern was that the children attending were running totally out of control with no one overseeing them. They were making service for the wait staff very difficult and you could feel the staff's frustration mounting as no one stepped in to manage the kids.

Then event planning disaster struck. The children began playing tag around the server who was in the process of carrying the wedding cake out to position it for photographs, and one of them collided into her. I watched the wedding cake tumble to the ground and land upside down. Luckily, the cake had been covered with a cloth to keep it from the guests' view until it was ready to be unveiled, and with careful maneuvering—keeping the cloth in place—the cake was able to be righted and brought back into the kitchen to assess the damage. The entire top of the wedding cake was damaged beyond repair. One guest set off to see if they could find a local bakery that would be still open but that was very unlikely as it was past closing time on a Saturday night.

I began to feel eyes focused on me to fix this problem—most knew what I did for a living—so that the couple could still take their wedding photos with the cake. Venturing into the kitchen I saw the chef, who was not a pastry chef, at a loss for what to do. To me, there was only one viable solution and I had one of the wait staff set off to bring me back one of the bridesmaid's bouquets to see if we could create magic with the help of some visual aids. And that we did.

The chef was able to create icing from ingredients on hand, a veritable miracle considering this was a catered event at a private venue so it wasn't a fully equipped kitchen, and together we were able to create a beautiful floral wedding cake topped with some of the flowers from the bouquet that—with the help of the icing—covered the damage that had been done. Up to this point the bride and the groom were unaware of what had taken place but when told and they saw the results they were delighted. From what we could see from the digital proofs, with proper ambiance lighting showcasing the cake, the pictures turned out fine. Neither the chef nor I are especially talented when it comes to flower arranging but together we pulled it off. Life as an event designer is never uneventful. Note to self: Remember to take a flower arranging course in the future.

WEDDING DAZE: Q&A

Training Your Event Design Eye

Q: How can movies, going to the theatre, etc. spark your creativity?

A: Going to the movies or attending live theatre can help grow your imagination and creativity and help to spark innovative event design. They are often filled with special effects that can be adapted and used in a variety of ways, e.g., seeing a movie where lasers are used to protect a valuable item can turn into a team-building event with team members having to work their way through a laser maze—helping one another—without setting off an alarm. Attending a live theatre performance will teach you about staging, lighting, the theatrical use of scrims and the different visual effects that can be achieved. And, you will see how best to strategically plan a dinner theatre event, identify a potential location where VIP receptions can be held, and discover ways that the theatre can be used as a venue to host a private performance, such as to serve a private dinner on the stage or do a product launch when the theater is "dark." And it will also teach you to look at what needs to be reviewed, such as the visual sightlines and how many seats in the theatre are actually usable and in good repair.

Event planners always need to be on the lookout for something new or something that sparks their imagination. It should be impossible to sit through a movie, watch a live stage production, or attend a concert or fashion show and not notice staging, lighting, timing, special effects and audience reaction to what they are experiencing. Your eye becomes trained to look for the good and the bad. And each learning experience, positive and negative, gets incorporated somehow into function sheets, pre-con meetings, contract negotiations and the like in the attempt to dot another i or cross another t on the event planning "to do" or "what not to do" list.

Assignment

Watch a movie or television show of your choice with event planning eyes and see what ideas for themes, food and beverage, entertainment, activities, etc. come to mind and assess how they could be used to create something new for an event.

Sources of Creative Inspiration

Q: What professional avenues are open for event planners to increase their event design knowledge and operations skills?

A: There are many opportunities for event planners to take their event skills to the next level. The industry publications and industry associations offer many opportunities to learn and to grow through attending meetings, trade shows and seminars and through attaining industry certification. (Special note: Industry publications, industry associations and certification requirements can be found in the back of *Marketing Your Event Planning Business*.) In addition, there are many specialty courses that are available through many different channels.

Added knowledge in sports, wines, cooking, flower arrangement, etc. are all valuable. Investing in learning golf, for instance, allows you to design a better golf tournament because you will be designing from a player's perspective as well as an event planning one, and the bonus is that you will be able to take part in golf events with your existing clients and potential new ones. Cooking courses, with top chefs or featuring a specific cuisine, may bring new ideas forward with which to wow event guests. For example, edible bowls have been done for years and are now a matter of course, but one enterprising chef took that concept to the next step and designed edible spoons (made tortilla style with corn) that were served with different toppings nestled into the spoon (but you would need to be careful with ingredient choice and serving timing to ensure a spoon wouldn't sit too long and become soggy and break). Such innovation gives partygoers something new to talk about.

Assignment

Review industry publications and industry association sites to see the range of opportunities to develop event planning on an ongoing basis. Also, list personal passions and pursuits that could be of value and the reasons why, as in the golf example.

CHAPTER

5 FROM CITY LIGHTS TO DESERT NIGHTS

Em and her team are faced with handling their first death on a program, on top of handling the ongoing hijinks of some well known attendees during their event. Help comes from a very unexpected source, which teaches them to be open to people growing, changing, and rising to the occasion when needed.

JANUARY 20

Ah, a program with reinforcements.

Our team, whose joint mission is to make the seemingly impossible possible and done with ease, is pretty amazing and we truly look forward to doing exactly that on each and every program. On this trip, along with Dee Dee, we have Troy, J.T. Marco, Yul, Myki, Vero, Jae and Lainy. Myki, Vero, Jae and Lainy are all top freelance program directors who have worked around the world with us—often out of country up to 300 days a year—and who are an integral part of our "working" family. Wills (who we are flying in to help run the program) is also on board. On-site we are a very tight and highly experienced team. We're so familiar with each other that running a program is like running a well-trained-for relay race—each of us could hand over/shift responsibilities to the next, knowing all would be expertly handled, with no one missing a beat and nothing being dropped. Daniela is at home at head office keeping things running smoothly in our absence and running "command central," tracking the flights our groups are flying in on and alerting us to any delays or problems encountered so our program directors traveling with the affected group on the final leg of their journey—we have them positioned in Dallas and Chicago to meet connecting flights—can quickly respond to any emergency situations.

We know this client and their guests well. Many of their participants have been on their programs for years. We've seen partners and spouses come and go, viewed pictures and heard stories of their children and in some cases, now their grandchildren, and looked forward with as much anticipation as they do for their programs to begin. We're excited to see their faces light up and to get to savor their reactions to what we've planned. The sepia-tone "wanted" poster invitation to the company's top sales producers set the tone for this year's event of having their best meet in the Wild West.

This event has many moving parts and we need a full crew to run it. It's absolute bliss after a week on my own with Diamond-Diva and no backup reprieve. Won't make that mistake again. I'm just here this time around to make nice and leave when it feels right.

Dee Dee is running this show with Troy, or BoyTroy as we like to affectionately call him. Actually, he gave himself the nickname and it stuck. BoyTroy is a play on "boy toy," what all his female clients seem to regard him as and nothing could be farther from the truth.

BoyTroy may be young but he is happily married to a wonderful woman and nothing he does ever gives off the slightest wisp of his having a lack of decorum. He is absolutely respectful to his wife and his marriage but that doesn't stop both single and married women—both company execs and their guests—on his programs from throwing themselves at him, not caring about the wallet picture of his wife that he happily passes around, asked or unasked, if he is trying to make a polite exit from a sticky situation. They choose to be blind to the wedding band that he wears proudly and never leaves his finger. At a couple of events we had to set up a buddy system just to make sure that BoyTroy was left unmolested by a few certain female execs who hoped he would take them from their boardroom to his bedroom as an added sales perk. And he is equally protective of us in return when the situation warrants it. To us, BoyTroy is like the kid brother everyone wishes they had, but apparently those on the make see him as something completely different.

On the flip side, Jake, our other star sales executive, thinks he's HOT and God's gift to women. Luckily for us, it seems he's not completely correct. No one is literally dropping at Jake's feet, although that did happen to BoyTroy. The wife of one of BoyTroy's client guests—a senior executive—did exactly that in front of her husband, and before BoyTroy could disengage himself, she loudly and drunkenly suggested that they meet up at the resort for a naked Jacuzzi. As can be imagined, the senior executive was none too pleased to have his wife making a fool out of herself and of him in front of his peers and his bosses. We later heard that they ended up divorcing, and that the husband knew BoyTroy had done nothing to encourage her actions. It was apparently the last straw for the senior executive as this kind of behavior had gone on before.

Guests often don't realize the impact they can have on someone's life personally and professionally when they forget the event that they are at is primarily business mixed with pleasure, and that their behavior will reflect directly back on the person who invited them. For some an open bar is like waving a red flag; they end up being a bull in a china shop, with reputations crashing everywhere.

Using the buddy system, we kept a close eye on Jake as well, but for very different reasons. So far, nothing Jake had done had come close to crossing the line but we—okay, mostly I—worried about what could happen if his joking overtures ever met with a yes. Dee Dee swears Jake is harmless and says that he'd turn tail and run so fast in the opposite direction that you wouldn't see him for the dust. Jake swears he is on the lookout for Mrs. Right but my intuition tells me he would not be averse to hooking up with Ms. Right Now if the opportunity presented itself. But Jake is aware of the company rules with respect to expected conduct and to the best of our knowledge follows those rules while on-site and representing our company. What happens in his personal life after a program has run is none of our business and in our industry a number of people do end up dating and even marrying their clients, participants and even local staff they have met on a program.

Jake's clients seem to love him, even his brassy style, and he has some big multimillion-dollar accounts. Go figure. Jake's clientele tends to lean towards blue-collar boys-and-their-toys and boys-will-be-boys manufacturers who are more than comfortable on site inspections asking Jake to take them or direct them to the best stripjoints in town or find them a fun companion—Jake usually recommends they talk to the hotel bell staff or concierge and stays clear of it from that point on. BoyTroy's client's are more high-end, white-collar folks on the financial, pharmaceutical and entertainment side, and did the same but usually more discreetly although not always.

BoyTroy was shocked at what had taken place during one site inspection to the Orient where he witnessed firsthand the previously unimagined talents and flexibility some young female "dancers" had and said, while his clients didn't want to leave, he kept his head down on the bar most of the time. Jake, on the other hand, was nonchalant about the fact that one of his clients wanted him to go visit a renowned club called Dirty Harry's in the Caribbean where reportedly anything goes and patrons were locked in once the show began. Those kinds of requests were frequent from Jake's clientele and he took it in stride, practiced discretion and never told tales, which is one of the reasons his clients loved him and booked with him repeatedly. With Jake as their sales rep, they knew their event would be a success and that there would be certain fringe benefits, that he wasn't adverse to sitting down and having a beer or several with them, that he loved racing—both cars and the horses—and that they would be safe under his care for their well-being while away. By contrast, BoyTroy's clients loved that he was a great golfer and were always asking him to be part of their golf foursomes, that he could play a good game of tennis and that he could recommend the best wines to go with a meal.

When BoyTroy's female admirers aren't throwing themselves at his feet, they've been known to cause other havoc. One hotel sales rep who was always all atwitter in BoyTroy's presence accidentally set our office on fire—a small fire but a fire all the same—when she brought her hotel's top chefs and wait staff into our office to cook breakfast for us as a holiday surprise. Of course, she wanted to be in charge of preparing or at least supervising BoyTroy's dish and wanted to make sure that it was cooked specifically as ordered, and she was going to serve it to him herself. Well, that plan had to be abandoned when, because her attention had been on BoyTroy and not where it was needed, and she knocked over a chafing dish with a lit flame that quickly ignited some papers nearby. She slunk out of our office that day deeply embarrassed, never to return.

The Barracuda, however, was quite different. There was no ploy that she left unturned in her mission to try and get BoyTroy alone. Unfortunately, The Barracuda was the person her company executives placed in charge to be assigned to work with BoyTroy in handling their event and they had no idea of her hidden wanton

side. By day she dressed demurely in classic suits buttoned up to the neck and in sensible shoes, with her hair pulled back unflatteringly, but at home she favored silk robes with nothing underneath and her hair and morals let down, as BoyTroy discovered "by accident" one night, not realizing that he had been caught in an elaborate setup until he made his hasty retreat.

The Barracuda, having heard that BoyTroy's wife was out of town and that he would be attending an upcoming supplier event, called the supplier and had herself added to the list of attendees. It was a sit-down dinner and she insisted on being seated next to her sales rep so that together they could discuss their program needs with the supplier's representatives. That was music to the supplier's ears and her request was readily granted.

The Barracuda then scheduled a late afternoon meeting with BoyTroy at her office the same day as the event, and as BoyTroy was preparing to leave, she asked him for a lift to the presentation as her car was in the shop and it wouldn't be ready until later in the week. Up until then he hadn't been aware that she was attending the event. BoyTroy, gallant as ever, offered to take her there.

At the end of the evening The Barracuda asked if BoyTroy would be a love and drive her home as it was only a short distance away and would not be terribly out of his way. This woman easily earned over six figures a year and could have well afforded to take a taxi. Feeling trapped, not knowing how to nicely tell a million-dollar client to find her own way home, BoyTroy did as he was asked, but talked up his wife all the way back. Dropping The Barracuda off, he was relieved to have gotten away so fast. He had fully expected her to invite him up for coffee, as she knew that he didn't have someone waiting for him at home.

Before he was halfway out of her gatehouse community complex's driveway, his cell phone rang. It was The Barracuda telling him that she had forgotten her briefcase in the back of his car, and asking if he would be able to bring it to her as she needed to work on what was in her briefcase tonight (this after BoyTroy had volunteered to courier it over rush first thing in the morning). When he arrived back at The Barracuda's, he found that in the few minutes since he'd dropped her off she had changed into a silk robe that left nothing to the imagination as it was only loosely tied—there was no doubt that she was naked underneath—had dimmed her lights, lit candles and poured two glasses of wine (one to thank BoyTroy for all his help). Barracudas are known for moving fast and that she did.

BoyTroy regaled us with the story of his harrowing escape the next day at the office, looking for advice on how to best handle the situation if it ever arose again. That part was simple; blaming it on the company lawyers was always an easy out and a true one. Employees, personally, and the companies they work with can be sued if a client is injured while they are technically on the job or even in transportation provided by the company such as a limousine, car service or taxi, and this is not limited to the event planning industry. One hairdresser giving her client a ride home was involved in an accident where the client was seriously injured and she was sued for millions, as was her company. When in doubt of how to get out of something questionable, always cite company lawyer policy.

Another time, The Barracuda was immovable around the fact that she wanted only BoyTroy and herself to go on a site inspection, which we knew was a bad situation waiting to happen. We artfully contrived to have one of our freelancers, Myki, meet up with The Barracuda and BoyTroy in the destination in a way that looked as though it was by accident, not a carefully orchestrated maneuver called "Saving BoyTroy."

Myki knew The Barracuda well, having worked several of her programs providing on-site translation for their out-of-country guests. Myki spoke eight languages fluently. She didn't necessarily broadcast that last fact and it was very interesting to find out what was being said in the behind-the-scenes supplier conversations; apparently, many people underestimated her talents and judged her solely on her disarming looks. Those factors, combined with her sunny disposition, warm and winning ways and can-get-it-done-no-problem attitude was an asset to any program.

The Barracuda's bosses adored Myki and specially requested that The Barracuda make sure that we booked Myki for any programs they had going. We knew that The Barracuda would not bite the hand that feeds her very expensive tastes and do anything that would cause her bosses displeasure, such as being ungracious to Myki, whom their guests loved having on their programs as well.

The Barracuda did her best to catch BoyTroy alone using her namesake's lie-in-wait or ambush approach, hoping to catch BoyTroy by surprise and did once, but that was on the plane before they arrived. The Barracuda started to make numerous excuses to get up from her window seat and seductively climbed over him to get to the aisle. Greatly alarmed after having this happen twice, BoyTroy then leapt to his feet in a display of gentlemanly good manners whenever she made a move to exit again and would only sit down once The Barracuda was safely back in her seat.

By now, both BoyTroy and Myki were growing wise to The Barracuda's voracious and predatory ways and were ready to checkmate her at every turn. Myki expressed her happiness at her luck in running into the two of them while she was waiting for her friend to fly down and meet her to start her vacation (which fictitiously was to start after BoyTroy and The Barracuda departed) and charmingly gushed about how she welcomed the chance to review their upcoming program with them since she would be the lead program director on this one and get to enjoy their company, saving her from the fate of having to sightsee and dine alone, and no, no, it was not an imposition on her time at all but something she was thrilled to be able to do (all said with tongue in cheek and appearing genuine—being a professional actor is another one of Myki's hidden talents). She stuck to them like glue as she was assigned to do.

The Barracuda knew she had been caught at her game and never made the same request again. She knew one way or another she would be thwarted from achieving her main objective, which was to be alone with BoyTroy and to make him into her personal boy toy. No chance of that ever happening. Having one of my staff, my company, my clients or their guests being thrown knowingly into a compromising position is not something that is ever going to happen under my supervision.

Starting out in the business, before I became savvy to the ways of the world, so to speak, I had found myself placed at personal and professional risk while entertaining business clients, who had a very different definition of the meaning of being entertained, while on-site or on a program. I remember how it felt as a novice one night in Europe, on a site inspection that I had taken alone with one of our top clients. I received a call from the inebriated company president telling me that he was on his way over to my room—he had obtained a key from the front desk—to make my last night in Portugal "memorable." It was memorable all right. I ended up pushing the heavy armoire in front of my bedroom door so that I could sleep soundly. The next morning I spoke to the general manager of the hotel and told him what had taken place the night before, as I had found out it was the duty manager that had given my key out to my client in an effort to placate him. I don't know if anything was ever done about it.

And another time I found that I had been set up to go on a private yacht cruise in the Greek isles (we were going to charter the boat for an exclusive executive retreat) alone with a company owner who had felt that one representative from our company—that would be me—would be sufficient. He had told me that his wife and another executive couple were going to accompany us, which was not the case nor had ever been the intention. A cozy tête-à-tête

just for two at his company's expense was the main objective; monkey business not company business was top of his mind.

So our tactical operation with The Barracuda was done in a blatant display of good business ethics, business etiquette and with business finesse in a way that was designed to protect the honor and personal and professional reputations of all involved. Along with saving BoyTroy from having to deal with unwanted advances, we were also protecting our client's employee from embarrassing herself, and whether she wanted it or not, we did have her best interests, as well as our own, at heart. Note to self: Their company *really* needs to offer a mandatory refresher course on sexual harassment in the workplace; suggest that is added to their next company meeting that is scheduled to cover new company direction, policies and procedures because The Barracuda's not the only one in that company who likes to work very hands-on. One of her male colleagues visiting our office once plopped himself down in Daniela's lap without warning and draped his arm around her, trailing his fingers up and down her bare arms in what he thought was a suggestive manner. Said colleague was soon picking up his bruised ego, as well as himself, off of the floor as Daniela firmly scolded him for his inappropriate actions.

I'm actually arriving before our advance team, which will be on hand to supervise move-in; set up and oversee airport arrivals, transfers and hotel check-in; and be in place before BoyTroy arrives with his client's top executives and their event assistants. I want to take the opportunity before everyone starts to arrive to check out a couple of new venues for future groups before getting caught up in the whirlwind of advance group preparation.

■   ■   ■

Bob, my favorite limousine driver in Tucson, as expected, was there on time to pick me up. It was so relaxing to settle into my limo.

This one had to be the longest and most lavish I had ever seen in the area and not a request that I had made—and it was white (DiamondDiva would have loved it!). Bob will be taking me around the next couple of days to do my touring and possibly on a post-program side road trip, done in event planning site inspection style, to Sedona to check out their luxury resorts and spas, as pampered well-being corporate getaways—mind, body and soul retreats—were a growing trend. The dramatic red rocks and nearby Grand Canyon would be an added draw, so Bob and I left catching up until then. Leaving the driving in Bob's capable hands allowed me to focus on taking pictures and making creative theme and event design research and development notes.

■　　■　　■

I'm really looking forward to this program. It has a lot of moving parts so all of our most capable hands are coming together to pull off another creatively challenging program. The last two we had done for this client—one in the Bahamas and the other in L.A.—still had them and their industry buzzing. Creating and flawlessly executing one-of-a-kind, meaningful, memorable and magical special events is what we are known for around the world.

Everyone *loved* the one-day surprise employee appreciation event their company threw for them on their company's 10-year anniversary celebration. All of their employees and their partners were whisked away in the middle of winter for a same-day tropical barbecue beach party. The plane ride down and back was wild. Everyone was in such high spirits from beginning till end. One minute they were up to their ankles in icy gray slush and in just a matter of hours were being totally pampered while relaxing on a pristine white beach surrounded by palm trees, playing in azure water, warmed by the sun, the rum and other

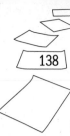

liquid libations, eating good food, enjoying great entertainment and living. For many it was a daydream fantasy, a day in the sun, having fun in the middle of a deep winter freeze with someone they loved. Beats employee appreciation pizza and beer back in the office all to heck.

Their last incentive was a jaunt to L.A. when the Oscars were taking place. On their first night, their company took over the hotel's penthouse presidential suite—which took up an entire floor and had a wraparound balcony that offered wonderful views of L.A. from all sides—and served up a decadent reception for their guests that was fit for Hollywood royalty and featured a private concert by a well-known entertainer.

They spent the second night on a film set making their own movie. They had a blast. The invitations to their evening's event had been mock film clapperboards and at the film site all of the participant had a director's chair with their name on it, which was shipped to their home when they returned. Professional makeup artists and stylists worked with the company's incentive winners to get them ready for their starring roles, while their partners and spouses enjoyed food and drink from catered tables and helped the winners with their lines.

The next night, all of the guests were taken by stretch limousines (booked, contracted and deposits paid well in advance of the official Oscar date announcement, thanks to the expert help of our well-connected DMC, who knew when Oscar Night was scheduled to take place before it was even announced) to their farewell gala where they were greeted by their own red carpet, which was set for dramatic effect with six-foot pillars with flames burning up to 48 inches high lined up along the walkway. Screaming fans and paparazzi on hand to welcome them added to their delight in the festivities for celebrating winning their company's top sales achievement award. During their reception, dinner and awards presentation, carefully edited live coverage of the Oscars was shown, with clips from the movies they had made the night before spliced in. Follow spotlights and live eye camera added to the excitement, as company winners made their way from their table to the stage to accept both their company's highest award and a mock Oscar to remember the night and their starring performance. After the awards ceremony, guests had the limousines at their disposal for the rest of the night. With their statues in hand, they set out to enjoy a Hollywood night in true star fashion, and the stories that came back the next day swept through their company and industry.

They enjoyed every minute of their trip, basking in their "15 minutes of being a company superstar" fame and the cachet of their company once again celebrating their personal and professional successes by having staged something truly special for them that set them, their achievements and their company apart from their competition.

I looked down the list of this year's attendees and smiled at some of the names. As always, the group had their resident bad boy. In this company's case, Simon Oh was his name, or I should say *"Ohhhhh!!! Simon Ohhhhh!!!* as he never tired of introducing himself, remarking that that's how "the ladies" usually say his name, alluding to his prowess in bed. Dee Dee rolls her eyes each and every time she hears him try to use his pickup line, but Simon is relatively harmless as bad boys go. For one couple, this will be their farewell incentive trip with this company, as they are retiring and turning their franchise business over to their daughter and son-in-law to run. It's nice that all four of them are able to travel together this time so the beloved retiring dad and his wife could say their good-byes to their fellow colleagues and have the opportunity to proudly introduce them to their branch's new owners, whom their peers had been hearing stories about for years.

The first night is going to be relatively light. Everyone will be tired from traveling and looking forward to some quiet time. A themed Mexican Fiesta reception on the hotel grounds is planned so that guests can make an appearance, have some drinks, sample some food, while background music plays, and feel free to leave as early or as late as they please after their company pres says a few words of welcome. With Mexico just 25 minutes away it's a fitting welcome theme. The "heavy" (enough food to replace a dinner) Mexican hot and cold menu will include:

MUSHROOM CEVICHE ON CORN CHIPS

Grilled Cilantro Pesto Chicken with Ancho Chili Glaze

Black Bean and Corn Salsa in Blue Corn Masa Cups

Rock Shrimp with Pico de Gallo on Cucumber

Mini Beef Burritos

Black Bean and Vegetable Burritos

Goat Cheese and Chorizo Empanadas

Chicken Empanadas

Crispy Red Chili Chicken Strips

Crab Quesadillas with Asadero Cheese

BROILED CHICKEN WITH ANCHO CHILE AÏOLI

Rock Shrimp Ceviche in Mesa Corn Cups

Spicy Crab Salsa with Tomatillo Medallions

Vegetarian Tortilla Roll

Cilantro Meatballs

Asadero and Roasted Pepper Quesadillas

It will all be served with icy Mexican beers, margaritas and other tequila specialty drinks, along with a traditional open bar.

JANUARY 21

This morning, guests were to enjoy a fun Jeep rally, which had been designed to introduce them to the beauty of the desert up close and personal, and end up taking part in a city slicker cattle drive on horseback, learning techniques they could use to drive sales back in the office, promote teamwork and develop quick decision-making and organizational skills. Then they would break into a hearty packed lunch and be given a custom steam-fitted Stetson cowboy hat. For those who didn't want to try horseback riding, other tie-in activities designed to impart the same learning lessons were going to be provided. At the end of the cattle drive, shuttle buses with beverages and snacks onboard would be waiting to take participants back to their resort in air-conditioned comfort.

Well, that was the plan at least. We failed to factor in Simon Oh and his band of mischief makers (all guys, some single and some who had opted not to take a partner on the trip) taking over a shuttle bus and trying to make a run for the Mexican border town of Nogales for some tequila shots, out-and-out frolicking, checking out the ladies of Nogales in their local strip bars and brothels, seeing the "Wet Dance" show they had heard about and investigating up close and personal not the desert beauty but the red light district, as the tearful staff member from the local DMC came to tell Dee Dee.

Trying was the operative word. Don't ask me how Dee Dee was able to cut them off at the pass. I did pass by once and overheard Dee Dee having a discussion with Simon about how Rocky Mountain Oysters or Prairie Oysters (fried calf and bull balls) are a delicacy and it would be her personal pleasure to have them prepared for him and his friends if he tried something like that again.

At least, I *think* those were the balls she was talking about having specially prepared and served up on a platter for them. I just kept walking and left everything in Dee Dee's hands. There could have been very serious consequences to their actions today, from being thrown into a Mexican jail to major financial legal liability to them, their company and the DMC if anyone had been injured on the commandeered shuttle.

My staff had been alerted to what had taken place but is well practiced in the art of discretion and schooled in the ABCs of event planning. Their actions and conversations left the guests none the wiser about Simon Oh and his crew's attempted shenanigans. In the client's and their guests' minds, Simon and company's late return to the resort was simply chalked up to mechanical problems encountered on their return shuttle bus and Simon was Ohhhhh, so grateful.

■   ■   ■

Diamonds and Denim is the theme for tonight's exclusive evening event being held at a multimillion-dollar Spanish Colonial estate that's nestled in the hills of the Santa Catalina Mountains. We love to use the estate when we are in Tucson. We've held so many events there that it's beginning to feel as though we're entertaining in our own home. Wishful thinking! The estate features grand mission-style architecture, lush landscaping, beautiful fountains, cobblestone walkways and waterfalls. The barns are filled with championship horses and also house extraordinary antique art and carriage collections. And there's a wonderful free-form rock swimming pool with cascading water.

Cowboy cocktails and appetizers will be served on the beautiful outdoor reception area, which is enhanced by willows and mesquite trees and is the perfect location to watch the sun set, listen to background music and stroll the grounds. Card sharks dressed in western garb, trick ropers and a friendly game of horseshoes will provide entertainment for the guests as they mix and mingle with their peers.

The estate's interior has saguaro-ribbed ceilings, hand-carved woodwork and a massive rock fireplace. A glass wall in the copper bar area opens to reveal an outdoor waterfall, making this the perfect setting for dinner and dancing. We're setting up the buffet outside to ensure good room flow, and that the guests get a hint of the beautiful grounds. The band we've hired is one of our favorites and we know that the guests will love their act. We've also hired professional dancers to teach those wanting to learn Tucson's popular line dances. The estate also has a beautiful fire pit and a hot tub as well, and s'mores, toasted marshmallows and a cowboy strumming his guitar under the stars will provide the finishing touches to the night.

Yum. Dinner tonight will consist of:

Vegetarian Chile with Sour Cream and Red Onions

Tossed Garden Green Salad with Ranch Dressing or

Cilantro Vinaigrette

Black Bean Salad with Roasted Corn and Sweet Peppers

Marinated Vegetable Salad

Penne Pasta Salad with Grilled Peppers and Herb Vinaigrette

Mesquite-Broiled T-bone Steak—One Pounder

Smoked Guaymas Jumbo Shrimp

Baby Back Ribs with Barbecue Sauce

Grilled Chicken with Sweet Barbecue Sauce

Ranch Style Baked Beans

Corn on the Cob

Baked Potatoes with Butter, Sour Cream, Scallions, and Bacon Bits

Cornbread with Honey Butter

Chocolate Pecan Pie

Warm Peach Cobbler in an Iron Skillet

Apple Pie

Sliced Watermelon

Coffee, Decaffeinated Coffee, Tea, Herbal Tea

Tucked out of sight, an area's been set up for staff to enjoy dinner as well, but not all at one time. The catering staff will prepare plates in the cooking tents and bring them over to our area as opposed to having our crew lining up with the guests. Joining the guests is just not done. Sometimes a client will invite the staff to eat with them but that's not something that we prefer to do. Having our own private, out-of-the-way area lets us catch up on what has to be done, gives us a break and lets us talk freely among one another without worry of being overheard. Beverages are kept strictly to soda, lemonade, sweet tea, hot tea, coffee, and bottled juices and water when we are working and even off duty, because you just don't know when you may be asked to round up a missing shuttle bus and a band of wayward men.

JANUARY 22

This year's gala farewell evening event and awards presentation should be another standout one for them and their industry. At sunset guests will be heading out to enjoy a hot-air balloon ride.

Chase cars will follow the balloons and take them to a champagne reception set in the middle of the desert. Waiters in tuxedos will be waiting with silver trays filled with the finest champagne while classical music is gently played, filling the desert air with haunting melodies to make hearts spill over with emotion. A large, clear tent has been set up. The decor and special effect lighting is breathtaking. A white-glove gourmet dinner will follow with a dessert presentation that is as pretty as it is delicious to eat. A cloud of spun pink cotton candy wrapped around ice cream with petals of sugared violets sprinkled around will be this evening's sweet ending.

Everything has been thought of, from heaters to take the chill off the night air and luxury porta potties, to astronomers with high-power telescopes to point out the stars that have been named after each guest—in celebration of the company's all-stars—from the Star Registry. A symphony under the stars will follow the awards presentation and with the client's blessing, not a desire to burn my client's money, a beautiful firework and laser display will be set to music as a grand finale.

■   ■   ■

It was an unbelievable night—an incredible success and the perfect send-off to the retiring couple who had helped the parent company enjoy tremendous growth in their early years. Guests were driven back to the resort in stretch limousines and can't wait to get back to the office to share their wonderful experiences with others.

But for us the night wasn't over. In the middle of the night we received a call that there had been a death on our program. The wife of the retiring gentleman had changed for bed happily talking about the wonderful evening she spent with her husband, daughter and son-in-law, closed her eyes, and peacefully died in her sleep. Everyone sprang into action and Daniela was contacted

back home. We need her to meet the woman's husband, daughter and son-in-law at the airport upon their return and do all she can to make this as easy a journey for them as possible. We have moved them to a different flight so that there will be time for us to make the necessary preparations on our end. It's the family's wishes that no one except the company president and as few people as possible from their group know what happened. Accepting everyone's condolences at this time would be more than they can bear and their wishes have been respected. They want to make the announcement in their own way and at the right time for them.

JANUARY 23

Myki and Jae were assigned to make sure that the family was looked after from that moment on and would fly with them and their wife/mother's body as well.

Being a master of discretion in event planning involves not only being vigilant and circumspect about the good and the bad that can take place on an event, but sometimes also the sad. Our hearts were breaking for the family. Our responsibility was both to them and to keep the integrity of the program as per the family and the client's wishes. Our demeanor could not change one iota until we waved goodbye at the airport to the departing client and their guests. It was essential that we kept up a good front with the rest of their participants—who were laughing, happy, revved up and ready to return home and work—as well as a professional one, which required us to focus on what we needed to do to have their program end on a high note for the other guests.

We couldn't allow our minds to center on what was taking place behind the scenes or relive memories of happier times, like when the couple had returned to the hospitality desk one year hand in hand, so excited to have climbed the Acropolis together. They recounted the story of how the man in front of them had inspired them—he was blind and climbing with a seeing companion and wanted to feel the joy of making it all the way to the top. They figured age was not going to stop them; if he could do it, they could—and did.

I knew that seeing them the previous evening, happily finding their stars in the night sky with the help of the astronomer—we had taken care to make sure they were grouped together—would be another lasting memory of the love they shared that I would carry with me. I hoped remembering hearing her say to her husband that now they would be together for all of eternity, which is all she had ever wanted in life once they met, would help console him and his daughter and son-in-law when they gazed at the night sky and stars at home. There was nothing the others on our team could do right now for them. Dee Dee, Myki, Jae and Daniela had the family under their protective care and everything under control and we could all rest easier knowing that. They had their job to do just as we had ours.

The only one from the group that the family did take into their confidence was, surprisingly to us, Simon Oh. He had amused the husband and wife with his antics this time (from their teasing remarks we gathered that they knew something about his shuttle escapade, but from him, not us) and in the past. It was a running joke that they were on the lookout for a good girl for him to settle him down. He stepped up amazingly to comfort them in a more personal display of affection than we could. Just goes to show you that you can never judge—or should judge—a person from one (or several) on-site incidents where bad behavior and impaired thinking can be set off by over indulging. You never know when they might live up to and even surpass your expectations. *Ohhhhh, Simon,* I think you won even Dee Dee's heart with the tenderness and caring you showed to this family, and for fully being there for them when they reached out to you, electing on your own to change your plans and fly home with them.

FROM CITY LIGHTS TO DESERT NIGHTS: Q&A

Event Planning Buddy System

Q: How does the buddy system work, when is it applicable and how does it affect staff scheduling and cost?

A: The buddy system is usually only in effect during events when an open bar is available to guests, when their inhibitions and professional and personal boundaries might get dropped. You usually know who is targeting who by that time. There are company executives and participants that believe that coming on to an event planning staff member is part of the package, and while they can be persistent but manageable during the day, they can get more out of hand once alcohol is added to the mix. Event planners need to be aware of what is taking place in a room and it's not limited just to the attendees' well-being.

Generally, an event is staffed so that there will be sufficient help on hand to manage any situation, which means staff to stay in the room, staff to get assistance if needed, etc., so it isn't about assigning additional staff to work together but rather to work as a team from their stations around the room and to practice safety measures, such as walking back to their rooms together (it's usually requested that staff rooms be on the same floor and in the same area as opposed to being spread out over the resort).

Assignment

Going back through the chapter, find one incident where the buddy system was needed and not practiced. (Answer: When the local DMC staff lost control of the minicoach and came to

Dee Dee in tears. There should have been a staff member on board each minicoach to travel with the group to make sure they were under control, especially after the drinking that had gone on at lunch. That particular staffing had been the responsibility of the DMC, but they had cut back on staff numbers without informing Dee Dee. She would not make that mistake again, adding that to her list of lessons learned.)

On-Site Codes of Conduct

Q: How is an on-site code of conduct established?

A: Before an event takes place, three pre-con meetings are held: one with on-site staff, another with the client and sales executive and a third with suppliers at the location. Before those meetings take place, each person will have received and reviewed the event's function sheets; the role they have been assigned to play, the timelines and event/show flow, dress codes, codes of behavior and codes of conduct are listed there. For example, the function sheet for the band will outline dress code; where they are to take their breaks and eat their meals; if they are allowed to mix with guests, drink or smoke while on duty; unacceptable language; the appearance of their instruments (e.g., no logos); and any other areas of concern. (Special note: Function sheets are covered in-depth in *Event Planning: The Ultimate Guide* and *The Business of Event Planning*.)

What qualifies as required and expected behavior can change from client to client, but what they are requesting must be in accordance with the event planning company's personal and professional codes of conduct, for instance, staff members joining the participants for dinner.

> **Assignment**
> Prepare a list of different areas of codes of conduct that could apply to staff, clients and suppliers that should be established prior to the event taking place.

Responsibilities and Boundaries

Q: Is there a difference between what BoyTroy and Jake do with their clients on site inspections? Is Jake breaking company policy by going to strip clubs with his clients?

A: Going to strip clubs with clients is something that Jake is comfortable doing, chooses to do and is not asked to do by the event planning company. Asking BoyTroy to do that would be inappropriate and could lead to sexual harassment charges. It is against his personal and professional code of conduct.

Jake does not actively suggest going to strip clubs but if in the course of an evening out his client wants to stop in for a drink at one, Jake is not averse to doing so. BoyTroy, on the other hand, handles the situation by ensuring that the client is in the watchful care of a DMC limousine driver if they want to set out on their own.

Each makes sure that their client is cared for and safe but staff are not asked to do anything that they are personally or professionally uncomfortable with. It is their choice. And they know that at all times they are a representative of the company and act accordingly. Successful event planning companies have set policies and their employees know exactly where and when to draw the line. During an event, sales reps are generally not assigned specific duties, as they require the freedom to be with their client and to do what needs to be done to service them. Client requests can range from personal to professional. For example, one company president wanted his sales rep to personally make sure that his wife and daughters were well looked after at a theatre event that was not part of the program.

Assignment

Name three situations where company policy, procedure and protocol should be clearly spelled out from a legal perspective and three situations where there is some flexibility, e.g., drinking while on program is not permitted but in some cases it may be in keeping with company policy for a sales rep to have a beer or glass of wine with dinner—if they choose to—with their clients while entertaining them on their site inspection.

Personal Drivers During Site Inspections

Q: How can you protect staff from bearing the responsibility of driving a client around on a site inspection?

A: It is always advisable during a site inspection or on program to have a professional driver and car hired to take care of the driving while staff take care of the client and the details. It is a time saver (no getting lost in a new destination, not wasting time searching for parking, etc.); enables the sales rep to have a drink at lunch or dinner with their client if they choose; and gives the event planning staff member, sales rep, supplier and client time to focus on what they are there for. It also works to ensure client safety, as an experienced driver can ensure you don't unknowingly venture into an unsavory part of town or a bar or nightclub that should be avoided.

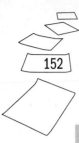

Assignment

Determine what costs need to be considered when adding to the proposed budget a private car and driver for a site inspection. (In addition to standard costs like rental, gas, insurance, and stocking the car or limousine with beverages and snacks, etc. there are often overlooked costs, such as meals for the driver—although that may not be a requirement on all programs—as well as tipping, and a buffer for overtime charges in case the evening goes later than planned.) Explain why a private driver and car is better than taking local taxis to get to and from your destinations.

Breaches of Supplier Codes of Conduct

Q: Should the night duty manager who gave Em's room key to her client have been reprimanded?

A: Yes. That situation needed to be addressed immediately with a higher-up but in this case the night duty manager *was* the one that had been responsible for handing over the key to the client, and at that time there was no one on duty that was in a higher position to deal with the matter. Still, the situation should have been brought to the attention of someone even higher.

Assignment

What other measures could Em have taken to feel safer that night as opposed to choosing to sleep in that room with a dresser pushed up against the door (which would not be safe in the case of an emergency that required her to leave the room quickly).

Adequate Staffing

Q: How could the minicoach takeover have been averted?

A: Having additional staff—experienced DMC staff—on board each vehicle, along with an event planning staff member, would have helped. They would have been on the watch for Ohhhh Simon's antics, which they would have already been briefed on. Assigning a young, inexperienced DMC alone to handle a group that had been drinking allowed Simon to take advantage. The learning lesson there was in future to have an event planning staff member as well as DMC staff onboard each motor coach, and to advise drivers to take instruction only from event planning staff members or DMCs. On this program there was enough staff on hand to have covered additional staffing on each motor coach, but having two events close together (the afternoon activity and the evening theme party) had split up the team numbers, as had scheduling time off for the staff who would be working the late shift and covering the evening event. There are times when it is necessary to work longer hours during an event or do split shifts to cover what needs to be done.

Assignment

Discuss other means that could have been used to maintain better control over the group with regard to return transportation if insufficient staffing meant an inability to have an event planning staff member aboard each minicoach. (Include increasing the minicoaches to full-size coaches or running manned shuttle service back and forth.)

Codes of Conduct on a Program

Q: Is it ever permissible for event planning staff to drink after hours when they are working out of country or on an overnight program?

A: This is an example of one issue that needs to be covered in an event planning staff code of conduct. It is up to each event planning company to establish what they will and will not allow and to ensure that their in-house staff and freelance staff are aware that the on-site job requirements extend well past an eight-hour workday. If all the event planning staff, in this chapter, had relaxed on the final night and celebrated by drinking, instead of preparing for departure day by doing final review of master accounts with accounting, going over luggage pull details with bell staff, etc., or been in bed asleep for an early morning shift, they would not have been in a position to respond as they did when they were advised of the death on their program.

You never know on-site when you will be required to handle an emergency situation, be it within the group or a national disaster. The time for celebration is back in the office when everyone is pulled together again for a post-event recap and discussion on learning lessons that can be incorporated into the next event to do it even better.

Assignment

Review different types of emergency situations that event planning staff could be required to deal with while handling a group that is overnighting in town, out of town or out of country, and make a list of different event planning staff—and supplier—codes of conduct that should be established.

Event Staffing

Q: When costing an event, should there be a standard number of event planning staff costed into advancing the event or will it change from event to event?

A: For costing purposes it is always advisable to include pre and post staff costs. You want to give the client a clear expectation of all costs with no hidden surprises at the end. Advance setup staff cost is an area that can be calculated by taking into consideration all that staff will be required to oversee, from pre-con to move-in, setup, rehearsal, arrival of group, group transfers, group registration (all pre-event activities), and teardown, move-out, and reviewing and obtaining final billing from suppliers (post-event activities). Some move-ins and setups can take a day, while others take a week or more. The same applies on teardown and move-out. And sometimes extra crew will be required to be brought in to facilitate a fast move-out if the facility has another event waiting to move in. It is advisable for event planning companies to establish a costing policy. For example, will pre and post staff costs be presented in the initial budget to the client or listed under "not included"?

Assignment

Using this chapter as an example of an incentive program, capture as many budget costs as possible that should have been included in the quote to the client. In which areas would it be beneficial to establish company policy?

Office Staffing During an Event

Q: Is it always a good idea to leave staff behind at the office or are there times when the office should be closed down and everyone take part in the event?

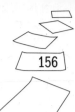

A: It is always advisable to have staff back in the office to attend to your other clients calling in, work on upcoming events and be there to handle any special requests or emergency situations. Experienced freelance event/trip directors are a valuable asset to any event planning company. Sought-after freelance staff can do research and development of an event in the office, step in and do event operations and work on-site around the world. They work for a number of event planning companies, unless they have an exclusive contract, and keep all that they do for others strictly confidential—their livelihood depends on their discretion. They can also teach event planning companies new, effective event execution methods that they have discovered while working around the world, or introduce planners to new ideas. In order to grow your company and your business, you need to grow your resources so that your company does not come to a complete standstill when an event is operating. Experienced freelance event/trip directors are very essential in helping event planning companies do multiple events at the same time.

Assignment

Discuss the various reasons why it is always advisable to have someone staffing the office while other staff members are out of the office running the events. (There are some examples in earlier chapters, e.g., monitoring the check-ins and flights on arrival day when the rest of the staff are either in the air with the group or on location preparing for them to arrive.)

Acquiring Knowledge

Q: Are there any other ways event planners and event planning companies can grow their knowledge?

A: Yes. This chapter presents many areas. For example, doing an event that includes fireworks and lasers gives event planning staff an opportunity to learn from experts in their field what has to be done, how it should be done and what could be done for even more impact. If you assign key personnel to manage these areas, you are also providing your company with a hands-on learning experience that can be shared back in the office and help elevate your company's knowledge. This will aid planners in event design and help them to be more creative in implementing tips and techniques picked up on the job while working with experts in their field.

Assignment
Discuss other learning opportunities included in this chapter.

Team-Building Group Activities

Q: Why wouldn't everyone be required to take part in the cattle roundup event on horseback?

A: Team-building exercises are wonderful for helping companies reach specific objectives, but the key to running successful team-building events is not to create personal and professional anxiety. Instead, create events that meet people where they are physically, intellectually and emotionally. Sometimes you can achieve that within the same event and sometimes it is important to stage a series of events that will produce the same result. For example, a flyfishing team-building experience was designed to give participants skills that transferred over to the office (e.g., learning to fish where the fish are), just as a yoga retreat was designed to develop skills that carried over to home (e.g., learning to push past discomfort). Both were set up so that everyone

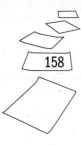

could take part, no matter their abilities. The same went for a ropes course where one part involved climbing up a telephone pole and jumping off (all safely strapped in). Guests learned to take one step more than they were comfortable with, and it did not matter if they only climbed three feet off the ground or reached the top. People learned regardless of where they stopped; the event was designed to give peer support and not be competitive. Horseback riding is not for everyone but there are ways to work with horses that all can take part in.

Assignment

Discuss the team-building lessons that could be used back in the office that would be imparted from a flyfishing team-building exercise, and look at how various team-building activities could be adapted to meet the needs of everyone, no matter their age or physical ability.

Using Special Effects

Q: When using special effects such as fireworks or lasers, what is important to keep in mind?

A: Always work with the best. Never choose your special effect suppliers by price but by experience, reputation and safety records. Make sure that all required permits and insurances are in place and up to date and that all fire marshal rules and regulations are strictly adhered to. In some cases you will be required to have emergency medical staff on hand, so be prepared for that request. You can't risk having unqualified people doing special effects. At one event using lasers, participants' eyes were damaged by too much intensity in the tent. The original event called to have the laser show take place outside but because of the weather it was moved inside. From newspaper reports, it did not sound as if adjustments were made to accommodate being in an enclosed space.

Assignment

Discuss various types of special effects that would require special handling. Several are mentioned in this chapter both in present and past events this group has experienced. (Special note: The six-foot pillars with flames burning up to 48-inches high would be considered a special effect.)

CHAPTER

6

INVENTIVE INCENTIVES

Em's innovative design creativity helps one company with limited funds meet their company objectives by developing a multi-tier program that has three events taking place at once in three different parts of the world.

FEBRUARY 14

Well, that went well. What a weekend. We had three identical events taking place all at the same time but in different parts of the world, and our client was soooo happy that we gave his employees and their partners exactly what they wanted and managed to pull it off with a reduced budget this year. Dollars the company usually spent on this annual event needed to be used instead to invest in expansion, but no one felt that they were taking part in an event that was not up to par with the past year's, which had been the goal.

Usually this client did over-the-top getaways for their top incentive winners and alternated each year between local, European and exotic locales. This year we did all three at once. This had been the year when traditionally everyone would have headed off to an exotic location but the dollars were just not there to be able

to take everyone. The client didn't want to send out a message to their staff—or their suppliers—about being concerned about costs and cutbacks. This was a year of tightening the belt, but they didn't want it reflected in how the top salespeople were rewarded. Pulling back the event and having it held locally would have raised red flags. The way to overcome this was to break the mold: move away from the old format and create a program that would meet their present budget needs, opening the door to doing something innovative and new again the following year.

When we looked at the dollars and the number of participants, what came to mind was doing a three-tier program. The top sales staff and their partners would jet off to an exotic locale, the next level would head to Europe and the last to a U.S. location, but each group would be experiencing the exact same life experience event inclusions on the exact same weekend. Each group became more intimate because of its smaller size. The employees loved the idea that they would get an opportunity to stand out from the crowd and shine and be able to spend quality time one on one with top company executives and their spouses, thanks to the smaller numbers per group.

All guests had their luggage picked up at their homes and whisked off to their destination. Their bags would be delivered to their guestrooms and be unpacked with all at the ready for them when they arrived. Limousines picked them up from their front door to the airport, where the guests flew away to a weekend of pampering, complete with custom monogrammed robes; couples' stone massages—with each partner also receiving training on how to give the other a stone massage (and a personal stone massage kit being delivered to their home upon their return); culinary delights at a private dinner cooked by a renowned chef for the region and served in a VIP section set up in their actual cooking kitchen; a top show complete with the best seats in the house, a VIP reception and backstage passes; and a private breakfast in a luxury department store before opening hours, where they were also presented with a shopping spree card and their own personal shopper to help them with their purchases before store opening.

It was wonderful that we were able to recreate the exact same level of life experience at each destination by doing it as a three-tier program to different destinations to keep the budget in check. No one felt as if they were not a true "winner," and back in the office on Monday they'll be able to share their different experiences with one another and create another motivational opportunity for the company. While the budget had been pared down, the experiences had not been and no one had the sense that this event design was the result of cost cutting while the company was going through expansion expenses. The company had now broken away from their old mode, bringing new energy into their incentive event program,

One last whoo hoo for pulling it off. Feels great when you can get a client to open their minds to new possibilities. This weekend event, held on Valentine's Day weekend, was perfect for the participants and their partners and gave them a romantic time-out for two they will long remember. Creating events that are meaningful, memorable and magical is what fuels all of us at the office. I'm very happy tonight that we hit all of the right buttons and made this work for our client and their guests.

INVENTIVE INCENTIVES: Q&A

Dealing with Budget Constraints

Q: How can you create effective event programs on limited funds?

A: Create one-of-a-kind—not cookie-cutter—life experiences that will educate, enlighten or entertain participants and give them something that they can take away that can enhance the quality of their personal and professional lives (like the couples' stone massages that were taken to a new level by also providing training on how to do stone massages on each other and having a kit sent to their home). It is not a matter of dollars and cents but dollars being spent to make sense and touch the senses in a way that will evoke the specific set of emotions that are required to achieve the results you are looking for. This can take place anywhere in the world and at any budget level. You just have to be open to new events and breaking away from what is traditional, tried and tired. People become blasé about taking part in a "been there, done that" event that offers no cachet and does not evoke either a personal or professional desire to experience.

Mastering strategic design is essential if you want to elevate the caliber of your events (*The Business of Event Planning* covers strategic design in great detail). One corporation credits the innovative well-being incentive program they put in place—which costs them $250,000 a year and runs through the year with top achievers in well-being (not sales) taking part in this particular incentive—with bringing them a financial return of more than $2 million dollars a year, and that is just the financial·return from lowered health insurance costs and other areas tied into that. Staff motivation is high, absentee-ism greatly reduced, staff turnover minimal and the energy of the company culture they have created by introducing this pro-gram is soaring—as is productivity—because what they put in place benefited their employees in their personal as well as their professional lives.

Assignment

Create a list of lifestyle life experience options at different budget levels that meet the criteria of being educational, enlightening and/or entertaining, as well as ones that are meaningful, memorable and magical. Remember, these can be fun or formal as well.

CHAPTER

7 ALL HAIL (OR OH, HELL) TO THE MAN WHO WOULD BE KING

Em and her team handle a difficult client on top of an intricate event program. They must devise ways to manage both successfully, making this a true test of their talents.

SEPTEMBER 5

This client is reminding me of the story of the emperor who wore no clothes but "his peeps" did not want to be the ones to tell him, and he is trying my patience. Jake has a client, a high-end manu-facturer, whose corporate, country and company culture is run very much that way. The events themselves are creative challenges—multimillion-dollar multimedia events filled with theatrical special effects and private performances with top-name entertainment with which to entice their dealers to attend and choose their event (and their product) over their competition's. We enjoy strategically designing and effectively staging them to bring about the desired return, but the client himself, The Emperor, brings with him his own creative challenges that test our patience, our endurance, our ethical business boundaries and our discretion.

Head Office is based overseas and The Emperor is here for a short—or long—reign, wholly dependent on sales results and the company's position in their marketplace. Their mission is to be number one and our mission is to help them achieve their goal by strategically using events as communication, marketing and sales tools. Unfortunately, our hands are often tied by the dictates of The Emperor and his band of solely male executives, whose livelihood and length of their own tenuous stay over here depends on how well they please this man each and every moment of the day and well into the wee hours of the night. Their fear of losing face and literally being sent packing with an imperious and dismissive "off with their head" is tremendous and very real as they have witnessed it taking place many times among their peers.

Jake was brought in to run and rescue one of their programs they were originally contracted to do with another event planning company who fell out of favor, and we only had a short time to turn around and craft something that would take them in a new direction and place them on the fast track to securing more sales. The other company was not producing results nor attendance and was deemed to be mismanaging company funds—by that The Emperor meant they were always coming in over projected "estimated" budget costs and had committed the ultimate transgression, one that caused them to lose the respect of their peers when one of their stage production's highly visible errors in judgment became known and fodder for their industry's gossip mills—through lack of discretion on the event planning company's part—and had everyone joking about what had taken place. (One of their top new products, long anticipated, billed as being a "powerful force" guaranteed to move the company forward, had to be pushed onstage during their product launch because of poor planning and logistical execution. No matter how much dry ice was used to try and hide the bunch of poor employees enlisted to push the piece of heavy machinery out on stage—instead of being powered under its own steam, as was the original plan, to great fanfare—everyone could see them and joked, "here's our hot new product but it doesn't work on its own and has to be sold with its team of manual workhorses"). Ah, the cost of doing business with an event planning company that doesn't know what they don't know.

Bidding for their business was, as usual, a feeding frenzy, with all the major event planning companies vying to be the one The Emperor selected. After the dust settled down and the incumbent event planning company had been selected to handle their upcoming event, they were ceremoniously rejected after coming back to the table one too many times with additional charges, and word finally getting back to The Emperor that what had taken place on their last event had gotten out. Enter Jake, stage left.

Jake just happened to make a sales call at the right time, with the right sample proposal of what we would do, an example of how we break down our cost summaries displaying our company policy of being one of total cost transparency, and being the right gender—a macho man, a manly man, a man's man, a ladies' man (even though just in his own eyes)—which was extremely beneficial as The Emperor and his peeps preferred dealing man to man and it greatly pained them to have to address a woman in our board meetings and on-site. Any of us of the female persuasion could be standing right beside Jake as he discussed event elements with The Emperor and his band of not-so-merry men and it was as though we didn't exist. There was no acknowledgement of our presence, and if the Emperor had a question to ask, it was asked directly to Jake, who would then turn to us for the answer, and then turn back to the Emperor and repeat what we just said. It was as though Jake was the female-to-male interpreter. And this would go on continually to all of our female amusement, which we did our best to hide. It didn't bother us, as we knew it was not personal nor a reflection of our abilities, just how The Emperor and his posse of men preferred to do business both here and at Head Office (that male–female condescension we saw displayed firsthand when they flew in to take part in their North American events). The opportunity to design spectacular themed multimillion-dollar events in which to showcase their product at their launches, combined with the chance to test our strategic event marketing talents to the max, more than made up for having Jake pull translation duty. While our competition had felt stressed to the max with them, we thrived on being stretched to grow and produce events that exceeded all expectations.

They had openly expressed enthusiasm for the example theme event, just one event element that Jake had shown them (their events traditionally went on for three to four nights depending on the location), so we had a feel for the style they were looking for and the message they wanted their product to convey to their dealers, suppliers and customers—that of leading the way to the future and that their products were the safest and best on the market. But to custom design an event that would bring them the company returns they were looking for and move them towards their desired number one industry position, Jake would have to work closely with them to create a past history and to get to know their intended audience's demographics. We knew he was capable of delving and digging until he got the answers we needed in order to give the client our very best, and Jake knew from experience that Daniela, who supervised planning and operations, would keep sending him back in until he did. The mock-up theme, with their delighted response, gave us a starting place. It was built around Inukshuks, the massive stone figures built in the image of a human that stand silhouetted on the treeless Arctic horizons erected by the Inuit people to serve as guides, giving direction to fellow journeyers and to all who would follow. They were a practical way of pointing to the better and safer way or passage. This really tied into their product. They were also symbols of showing responsibility and dependence on one another to make the way better and safer for all. And that expressed what they wanted their company to stand for.

IMAGINE . . .

The doors open. The room is bathed in darkness, completely draped from ceiling to floor in black. Steam rises from the floor, creating an atmosphere of stillness and the mists of the Arctic tundra. Twinkling everywhere against the black are hundreds of white lights and multi-colored moving curtains symbolic of the majestic northern lights. Lasers flash upon 15-foot Inuit stone sculptures standing guard over the night. The sound of a drum echoes in the darkness.

Tables are snowy white, accented with icy white neon and accent tones of icy blue. Each napkin is tied with icicle napkin rings and in the center of each table is a circlet of small inukshuk figures around glowing blue candlelight. At the end of the evening, each guest will take home an inukshuk figure as a memento of the night and a reminder of the power inherent in their ability to guide others (to buy their product was their ultimate goal).

The dinner: a delicious sampling of native offerings, beautifully presented and elegantly served.

When coffee and liqueurs have been served, a pool of blue light will appear on stage and the voice-over will introduce an award-winning singer for a private performance. A chorus of children's voices will be heard around the room. They will enter from the back of the room and make their way to the stage. The theme song written especially for the occasion touches on "wheels of change" and how together all of our dreams can come true. Guests will be carried back to the meaning of this evening's symbol—the Inukshuk and how it stands as a directional marker guiding the way—representing the responsibility

they share to one another, their dependence on one another and the importance of making an effort today that will make the way better and safer for everyone. Performance will also include Inuit dancers and drummers.

INVITATION

Custom invitations will incorporate a description of the inukshuk and the meaning behind the statue as it ties into the evening's theme. Custom menus will also carry the theme.

DECOR

- Inukshuk figures around the room with their product dramatically lit beside each one.
- Inukshuk figures (two) set to each side of the entrance that will become platforms for two drummers.
- Further treatment at each inukshuk location to include blue mini-lights and acrylic shards for shattered ice effect.
- Indoor pyro to simulate cascade of snow falling as the doors open.
- Snow blanket for base of inukshuk figures. Foam snowballs.
- Floor-to-ceiling black drape with stars and simulated northern lights effect.
- Bar areas: "glass block" bars enhanced with blue lights.
- Fiber-optic shimmer curtain for stage area with "iceberg" stage set. Stage for announcement and for high-energy dance band to follow private performance.
- Center revolving stage for performance, creating a "theatre in the round" atmosphere.
- Wall of ice lit with blue lights. Theme could be carved into ice block.
- Laser show. Dramatic lighting and special effects.

TABLE TREATMENTS

Combination of neon table treatments to include:

- Full-circle neon table tops with cloths placed over the neon piece to diffuse the light.
- Neon pedestals, high, as base for florals (white on white) or smaller inukshuks.
- White-on-white linens.
- Pale "ice" blue napkins with icicle and ribbon accent.
- Randomly strewn acrylic ice cubes in various stages.
- Glass-block pedestals for florals set on full neon tabletops.
- White chair covers with silver or pale blue ties.
- Cobalt blue glassware and plates.

PLACE CARDS

An engraved compass with each guest's name is used as a place card (tying in with theme: direction/leading the way).

The Menu

- Butternut Squash Soup (with a trail of roasted pumpkinseeds laid across the top)
- Choice of:

> Grilled Salmon with Rose Hip Sauce & Smoked Oyster
> Potato Cakes
> Roasted Turkey with Cranberry Pinion Sauce
> Buffalo Brisket Barbecue with Grilled Corn with Chili Oil
> and Pico de Gallo
> Venison and Ribbons of Summer Squash with Sage Pesto
> Custom Baked Miniature Alaskas

- Plates will be dusted with paprika in the shape of directional markings—north, east, south and west—and set upon juniper or pine branches.

Take-Away Gift

Autographed CD.

Optional Enhancement

Existing lights can be changed to icicle light fixtures.

There were learning curves along the way but we skillfully ma-neuvered our way through them. Jake more than did his part; he stepped "manfully" into his role and grew close with The Emperor and his band of not-so-merry men. We learned over the years:

- That the key to winning the account year after year—yes, the feeding frenzy still went on, as it was Head Office policy to get comparison quotes in and you couldn't take it professionally or personally—was winning The Emperor's heart by suggesting only destinations that offered access to world-class golfing, gam-bling, water-skiing and deep-sea fishing. A combination of all of the above was highly desirable but any one or more was a guar-anteed yes. And suggesting a location, no matter how perfect for the participants, where The Emperor had family with whom he would then be obligated to spend time, was a definite no.
- That it was imperative that The Emperor be booked the best suite in the hotel or resort and that no one be booked on the same floor as he was or be placed on a floor numbered higher than his was. Ideally, finding a hotel or resort with two towers made that logistically easier on guestroom managers.
- That not all women were treated as though they did not exist. We were asked oh so discreetly to hire a specific young lady, Sandy, The Emperor's close "friend," as a "freelancer" to be on each and every event program and to be assigned to fly with The Emperor on his private jet and to accompany him in his private limousine when and where requested. MistressSan-dy was allowed to dress as she pleased, do as she pleased and

work exclusively for The Emperor to tend to his, um, personal needs when she was requested, no matter the time, be it day or night cough cough—summonedtohisbedroomorelsewhere—cough cough (really have to do something for this tickle in the back of my throat) and to never mention to his wife, who sometimes accompanied him on his trips (depending on quality of upscale shopping available in the destination), that Mistress-Sandy did not work for us full time. "I knew she would be sporting a 'tramp stamp,'" Daniela declared with a righteous sniff the first time she saw MistressSandy in a barely-there bikini with her tattooed backside. Must say The Emperor paid her well—we saw MistressSandy's "salary" that was approved and written into his company event budget, as were all her on-site personal credit card and signed-to-the-room charges. I must say The Emperor's female conquests certainly liked to shop and pamper themselves. It was difficult to say who spent more when they were both on these trips—MistressSandy or The Empress. Jake hated the trips when The Empress was on board. It became his duty to escort her where she wanted to go, as The Emperor only felt comfortable with her safety when Jake was there to take care of her needs. Translated, that meant The Emperor knew Jake would check in with us to alert us when The Empress was returning so that we could inform The Emperor's entourage of men, who in turn made sure that The Emperor was not caught without his clothes. Only once was there a near slipup when Jake called in a little too close to the resort and The Emperor's posse almost broke their necks trying to get down the escalator as fast as they could to greet the returning Empress and delay her on her way to her suite. A senior executive from the group was sent to alert The Emperor in the agreed manner, returning to our hospitality desk visibly shaken, panting from his race to goodness knows where, and apparently in desperate need of a stiff drink to recover his

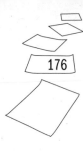

nerves as he requested the key to the private executive bar suite.

- That The Emperor loved our added touch at casino destinations of having casino dealers that spoke his native language brought in for their stay.

- That you have to specifically request "clean rooms" be given to guests checking in at some casino resorts and hotels around the world, as they would prefer guests out of their rooms and gambling instead of relaxing and settling into their suite, and have been known to check guests into rooms that have not been turned around from their last guests, which forces the new guest out of their room and into the hotel—hopefully spending money—until their rooms have been cleaned.

- That a car can explode in an underground garage when it reaches a specific heat and the windows are rolled tightly shut. Luckily it wasn't the car holding a supplier's much needed equipment. We thought The Emperor's posse moved quickly when The Empress returned unexpectedly early—should've seen how fast Dee Dee and the rest of her team made it to the garage when they heard what had happened to the car and they knew it was parked in the general vicinity of the supplier's.

- That no matter how much care is given, sometimes during an event a fire can break out. It wasn't at The Emperor's table but it was sure close, as it was the table that had been originally assigned to him. During preparation for the product launch our audiovisual and special effects team had done everything in accordance with fire marshal and hotel regulations around fire safety. All materials being used were treated with fire retardant, etc., as per requirements, with official certification and permits obtained. The indoor pyro we were using as part of the grand finale production number went off without mishap but it was the hotel's own crew, who were known for being masters of illusion and magic, and their confetti that was supposed to be flame retardant that caused the fire at dinner during one of their stage numbers, when the confetti burst went off too soon, triggered by someone playing around backstage, and confetti fell heavily in a clump on lit center-pieces—candles that were going to be removed after coffee and dessert. The confetti, something the hotel used on a daily basis and supposedly fireproofed to within an inch of its life, went up in flames. The official fire watch marshal hired by the hotel to oversee the event did not catch what was happening and it was BoyTroy to the rescue (we made sure we brought male reinforcements on all of The Emperor's programs). He alerted the serving staff who quickly, quietly dealt with the matter and reset the table.

- That we endeared ourselves to The Emperor's posse when we helped one of their members save face and they never forgot it. The thank-you gift to The Emperor, which he loved, was a limited edition item that had been very hard to obtain and that Jake knew that The Emperor would cherish. It was entrusted to one of The Emperor's men to hand-carry home with him and present to The Emperor back in the office the next working day, even though we had previously offered to take it back with us or have it sent directly to his office. The Emperor's entrusted servant—oops, I mean employee—lost it checking in at the airport. He called us, frantic, from the airport, from the plane, from the connecting airport, from the plane, begging us to find an alternative, have it engraved with the exact same plate and message and bring it to him at his home the next day. And "don't ask me how" Dee Dee, when the hotel staff said it couldn't be done for at least two or more weeks, was able to do exactly that. Although I did hear rumblings, or were they grumblings, about the hotel's general manager being tracked down while dining out with his wife and friends in another

state, permission being granted to have hotel security break into his private office to get a duplicate—the general manager's own prized possession, which is where Jake had got the idea in the first place for The Emperor's gift—carefully removing the personalized plaque, tracking down another, having it engraved, packaging and placing it in Dee Dee's hands before she had to set off for the airport. The next day the package was delivered safe and sound into the very anxious arms of The Emperor's most trusted man. Dee Dee said his gratitude made her eyes leak—she would never willingly admit to being moved to tears by one of The Emperor's men. It was our pleasure to have been able to have pulled that off. We knew how important it truly was to that man and were willing to do whatever it took to make it happen and happen on time.

- That in return for our kindness that day—we were in tight now with The Emperor's men as we had saved one of their own—we learned what we had long suspected was true: that The Emperor's boardroom/meeting room was bugged and had two-way mirrors, and that it was a ploy to have company executives leave the meeting on one pretext or another and leave visitors or company employees not in the know (not part of The Emperor's inner circle and privileged posse) alone to see what they would do or say during the calculated absence.

- That the world—our world—must come to an immediate grinding stop when one of the King's, I mean Emperor's, men called in with a question. They were insistent, the questions incessant, and they needed an immediate response in order for the calls to stop coming in. The Emperor's posse were not doing this to drive us insane, although that was Daniela's personal take on this matter when she crossly voiced her opinion after intercepting one too many calls one day, or at least the theory she shared with us aloud. I have a good idea of what else she might have been muttering beneath her breath. They merely were looking to have every conceivable answer to any possible question that The Emperor could ask in a meeting. They did not want to be called upon and not have an answer ready so they prepared for that eventuality by calling us. *They* had absolutely no problem dealing directly with women when Jake was nowhere to be found. Their fear of losing face in front of their colleagues and The Emperor was greater than not wanting to get an immediate response from a female, especially since they now knew they could trust us to do our best for them personally and professionally, but of course none of their cohorts could know that the other had called and putting out a memo outlining all for everyone was unthinkable (from their end). Sighhhh . . . what we do and have to put up with sometimes in the name of discretion, customer service and good business can be very revealing about human nature, corporate culture, what people value and where they place their values.

- That it is possible to fly to Las Vegas and back in one day, do a full day's work *and* taste test, as per his request at some restaurants that featured The Emperor's favorite national foods "just in case" The Emperor had a craving that needed to be met and to make sure the selected restaurants would meet The Emperor's personal preferences and standards.

- That The Emperor wants to personally meet every top-name talent after they perform and requests that they come to him. Most comply but one performer—a male—would not. He requested The Emperor come to him. There was a standoff and neither's ego would allow them to give in. Dee Dee came to Jake's pleading rescue; he was getting tired of running back and forth negotiating what would take place. Dee Dee set up a private meeting between the two "men" at the exact halfway point. This and all other concessions must be addressed and agreed upon and written into contracts before they are signed.

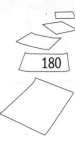

- That if Head Office elects to fly over and attend an event, expect the whole company—theirs, not ours—to be thrown into a pleasing tizzy the likes of which we have never before witnessed. Over 27 versions of a name badge had to be made for The Chairman in the event that he decided to wear a name badge (*as if* everyone wouldn't know who The Chairman was, surrounded by his procession of men in front, beside and following behind him, making every entrance a grand entrance—and here we thought The Emperor's entourage was large—and *as if* The Chairman would ever elect to wear one, but hey, if he did we had very conceivable variation of how he might like his name and title to read).

- That The Chairman would not go onstage to speak unless a very specific brand of men's hair care (not found advertised here since the late '60s) was found and brought to him. Try scouring a foreign city for that early one Sunday morning, but our local DMC didn't fail us. American Express is the card that says "don't travel without it," but we never left home without a certain product—when doing The Emperor's programs—because you just never know when a little dab will do you, or do you in, as the case may be. Both Daniela and Marco were horrified at what The Chairman was electing to use and longed to bring his hair care into this century.

- That each year a brand new, bright, eager–for-promotion sacrificial employee would be hired and assigned to work with The Emperor's men to do the mountain of work that was part and parcel of putting on an event. Each project manager was determined to break the job assignment's curse of being fired after the event had taken place, but, alas, none was employed the next year to tell the tale. It didn't matter how hard they tried, how late they stayed—they were used up and dismissed on one pretense or another. Their real role was not to be designated project manager, but to be "fall guy or girl" or "fall-on-your-sword guy or girl" in the name of protecting The Emperor's men in case something triggered Head Office's or The Emperor's displeasure. Someone had to be dismissed, and The Emperor's men knew that it was not going to be one of them if they could help it. When the new project managers would ask about those who had fallen before them, it was our job not to enlighten them but, without telling tales out of school, to help them do all possible not to lose disfavor. For example, just because we now knew with certainty that their company meeting room was miked didn't mean that it was our place to tell them, but we could steer the conversations to safe topics when left alone with them during event planning meetings.

- That you should never ever expect to see your room when on program with The Emperor. No matter how longingly you may look at the sunken bathtub located right next to your bed overlooking the city lights, your luxurious suite, which your sales manager assigned you in the hopes of winning future business, will merely become a place to shower and change clothes, and maybe, just maybe, catch an hour or two of precious sleep. More appreciated would be a room close to the ballroom so we could perfect the art of being quick-change artists. Yul remarked wistfully one day, but just teasing, during setup when we had been pulling 20-hour days, that he had heard there was an amazing theme park nearby. A deep longing sighhh for time to play. But Yul was totally committed to staying until what needed to be done had been completed and we could all call it a night. Jake, on the other hand, hoping to escape notice and have a moment's reprise from ending up with The Empress duty, turned off his cell, his pager and his walkie-talkie—a no-no in our business—but he forgot to turn off the tiny live cameras that key staff members were assigned so that Daniela, set up in the hotel at command central, could monitor what was taking place during move-in, setup,

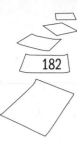

rehearsal, day of, teardown and move–out, and dispatch people where they were needed. Jake was found in a matter of
minutes much to his dismay, and Dee Dee took great pleasure
in personally escorting him to where The Empress was waiting
for him to take her out and about.

- That we must be able to cost an event down to the exact penny.
Spend one nickel—and that is not an exaggeration—more than
"estimated" and there was hell to pay finding out exactly where
and why that nickel went. The Emperor's men could happily
spend hours of company time looking for the elusive nickel
and we didn't have time to play that game, so our costings
were so precise that even The Emperor was impressed. And,
in turn, we helped our suppliers to grow better at pricing. We
fully understood The Emperor had been burned in the past and
that was something we could make sure never happened again,
as pricing, along with creative design, is one of our strengths.
The event planning company that misspent in the past for a
custom-designed cirque-style show—we could not believe how
little they knew—had totally forgotten to question, let alone
cost, the type of flooring the acrobats needed, how the rigging
worked, how long would it take to put up the rigging, what the
weight system would require, green room and dressing room
setups, having seamstresses in place to handle any last-minute
adjustments, the costs to have all the costumes and equipment
brought in, blocking in and including costs for dress rehearsal,
finding out if the hotel was unionized and what that would
add to the cost, and why 50 people were coming down for
a 10-person act (some of them were children of the performers, which could be a rider condition, but at least they should
have known it and cost it going in). They even proposed something totally impossible with a prototype, not understanding
just how fragile it is. And that was just one event component.
No wonder The Emperor and his band of men looked with

mistrust upon those they were doing business with until they won their confidence. But part of being masters of discretion means not trashing your competition to clients, suppliers or anyone else in the industry and letting others know the other company's Achilles' heel. That we kept to ourselves, but Jake went on a mission with single-minded determination to land as many of their accounts as possible using what he now knew to his sales advantage but without giving anything away, looking to save other clients from a similar fate.

- That it was to our advantage to bring down as many men from our team as possible in the event that Jake was not in the vicinity and The Emperor or one of his entourage needed to speak to us and required female–male translation services performed. Back in the office the entourage had no problem calling and speaking to us directly, but on program with The Emperor or his other many followers around it just wouldn't happen. It was a game of follow the leader and we all knew it wasn't personal, just a part of their corporate culture.

SEPTEMBER 14

Still here overseeing teardown and move-out of the client's product with some of their executive staff and just heard that for their next event The Chairman is flying in and bringing his wife and his children, who he is placing in Jake's tender care along with The Emperor's Empress. Time to check our hair product stock and see if we can find a resort that offers three separate towers. Have a feeling Jake is going to be one very busy person. Note to self: Have Daniela look into those new running shoes that come equipped with a GPS tracking system for Jake, and make them part of Jake's required dress code for the event while move-in, setup and rehearsal are going on. It'll be our little secret in case Jake attempts any more disappearing acts.

ALL HAIL (OR OH, HELL) TO THE MAN WHO WOULD BE KING: Q&A

Client Culture

Q: Why is it important to understand your client's corporate culture?

A: Knowing your client and their attendees allows you to design an event that will be a match for who they are. It is important to know the group demographics and corporate culture as well. If they are formal, a playful event will not sell. If they want cutting edge, because of the nature of their company, their profile, their platform and their positioning in the industry, they will not want—nor should you ever deliver—a cookie-cutter event.

Assignment

Discuss ways you can pick up clues to a company's corporate culture. Some are visual, some are spoken, some are in actions required of them and required of you.

Costings

Q; How is a costing best presented to a client?

A: Event planning companies present their costs to clients many ways. One way is by "packaging" the event, presenting one price (either a total or a per-person cost) to the client. Another way is to lay everything "menu" style and to add a flat management fee or a percentage management fee based on the total cost of the event. It is important for an event planning company to set company policy and procedures with how their proposals and cost breakdowns are to look and be laid out so that there is uniformity. That will reflect on how your company does business, e.g., it shows you have an eye for detail.

Assignment

Discuss the advantages and disadvantages between the two cost breakdown styles and how each is impacted when clients make changes, such as to guest numbers, and which will allow the client to make better informed decisions. Using the theme party ideas in this chapter, look at different ways the costs for this event inclusion could be laid out and presented to the client.

Proposals

Q: How many proposals should an event planner prepare for a client?

A: The objective is to select the best event to meet the client's objectives and not offer them a smorgasbord of options. They are coming to you for your expertise, not multiple choice. Research, development and proposal preparation is costly in terms of time, energy and money, and many event planning companies submit proposals "on spec" with no guarantees that they will receive the business. When all costs are factored in, preparing a proposal can come in over $10,000. Some event planning companies have started to charge a fee for proposal preparation, which is applied to the event once contracted, and other event planning companies refuse to get involved in bidding wars. That seems entirely reasonable when you consider that one client was known to solicit up to 19 bids for their events.

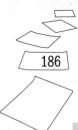

> **Assignment**
>
> Create a proposal for a client presentation, tracking the number of hours spent on preparation and costs involved (hours, long distance, couriers, etc.).

Proposal Costs

Q: With the high cost of creating a proposal, how do you select the right event without covering all your bases?

A: It is important to qualify a client's proposal request, and that means obtaining specific answers to specific questions. Many event planning companies design client proposal request forms that are mandatory for their sales staff to complete with their client before a proposal will be prepared. If a client does not have the time to help you design the best program for them, you need to question whether or not they are serious about holding an event or if they are merely shopping around for ideas and planning to do the event themselves.

> **Assignment**
>
> Design a client proposal request form that will better help you to create an event that is the perfect match. Use some of the material from this chapter to help you. Hint: Refer to what was learned from past events.

Client Protocol

Q: Is there anything that an event planning company can do should they run into a client who will not do business with some of their employees, as in the example in this chapter?

A: In this chapter, the decision to prefer working with males is part and parcel of their corporate culture and it still exists today. You can win them over slowly, but there may be areas of compromise in the beginning and perhaps forever. It is up to the event planning company and their staff to decide if they want to proceed and if they can handle the demands of a certain client.

Assignment

Discuss ways that event planning companies can handle clients with very specific service needs and how to decide if and when it is time to walk away.

Client History

Q: Along with the client proposal request, is there anything else that will help an event planning company zero in on what event elements to include?

A: Preparing a client history is another vital peace of information that planners will require in order to be able to select the appropriate venue, event elements, etc., and it is important to know what worked and did not work.

Assignment

Create a client history template that would give event planning staff the information they need to begin preparing a proposal. Use some of the material from this chapter to help you. Hint: Refer to what was learned from past events.

Client Proposal Requests vs. Client History

Q: What is the difference between a client proposal request and a client history?

A: A client proposal request is focused on the upcoming event. A client history is what actually took place in the past.

> ### Assignment
> Think about who else besides the event planning company can benefit from knowing a client's event history and why.

Special Requests

Q: Can company policy be established on how to handle client "special requests"?

A: Company policy needs to be in place and all employees—in-house, sales and freelance—need to know where the line must be drawn, what will be condoned and what will not, and how to deal with such requests with tact and finesse.

> ### Assignment
> Discuss the situation outlined in this chapter with the client wanting to have his mistress hired as freelance staff, with her salary built into his program and paid for by his company. Are there legal ramifications? Are there moral issues and will staff morale be affected?

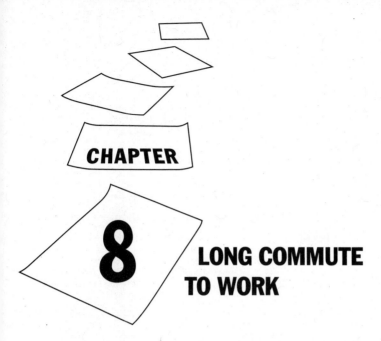

CHAPTER

8 LONG COMMUTE TO WORK

Em sets out on her own to do a site inspection for a client and then heads to a nearby destination to check it out as a possible incentive destination for other groups. Her trip includes a few surprises.

SEPTEMBER 16

Another day, another country. Getting on a plane to go to work for those in the international corporate, social and celebrity event planning business feels exactly the same as getting in the car, on the bus or on the subway does for others, except you sometimes have jet lag and heavy baggage to contend with. Next trip we're using Luggage Forward, where they pick up your luggage at home and when you see it again it's in your hotel suite, and at the end of your stay you can either send it forward to another destination, back home or to the office, which sounds simply blissful. It worked very well with our three-tier group program, and we need to take just as good care of ourselves as we do of our clients. If Dee Dee has her way, all our overnight flights will be on private jets or luxury airliners like EOS Airlines, where the airline seat turns into a private airline suite when it's converted to a six-foot bed. The poor girl had been emotionally scarred after waking up on an

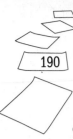

overnight flight to find a teenage boy snuggled into her, drooling happily. Daniela has volunteered to do any overnight flights where she can board Singapore Airline's newest aircraft, with the full sleeping suites.

I remember waking up many times wondering where in the world I was—seriously! When I do that and find I'm home in my own bed, I know my trips are running too close together. I don't know how some of the freelance staff do it, traveling up to 300 days of the year.

I don't think I really realized starting out just how much traveling I would be doing locally, nationally and internationally. You end up traveling a fair bit not just on site inspections to run the client through the event and going on-site for the event but also on fam—or familiarization—trips as well so that you can check out new destinations and resorts to see if there is a fit for your clients. Fam trips can take a few days or a couple of weeks, depending on where you are traveling to. Sometimes when you find yourself in a part of the world that you know holds great appeal for incentives, meetings, etc., you tack on a couple of nearby destinations to check out at the same time in case you want to consider them as destinations on their own or as part of a two-tier program.

Some days the commute is just a little longer than others and today was one of them. It took me over 36 hours to reach Mauritius. I felt I had become one with my seat by the time I finally arrived. I was on a site inspection but entirely alone as the client was leaving it up to me to make the decision for them as to whether or not it would be the perfect spot to travel to after their upscale African safari next year. And it was. BoyTroy and Dee Dee already had done the African safari site with the client earlier this year and everything was set there. Mauritius was an add-on program they had decided to do as a post executive retreat and wanted it checked out as soon as possible. I was already scheduled to travel to the Seychelles for another client site inspection so I took Mauritius on as I was going to be in that part of the world anyhow. BoyTroy and Dee Dee were off running this year's event for the client and could not join me, so it was just me, myself and I to enjoy the island at my leisure and getting to set my own timetable. But after just coming off The Emperor's program and traveling all this way, the only thing I wanted to see at that moment was my bed.

I was very grateful to see my limousine driver waiting for me when I cleared customs, and the drive to the resort was uneventful. I wasn't in a space to truly take in what I was seeing and appreciate it, let alone evaluate it. That I would do tomorrow. My first priority when I hit my room was a shower and then sleep.

The resort was welcoming and my suite was gorgeous. I felt like a pampered but very tired princess. A selection of refreshing tropical juices on ice and a light repast of local specialties was waiting for me in my suite, and I looked forward to sampling local cuisine when I arose. The hot shower had been refreshing and my bed looked so inviting. Wrapped in the resort's sumptuous robe I prepared to lie down. Just as my body was starting to relax I opened my eyes one last time before I succumbed to sleep and was out of that bed so fast I surprised even myself as well as the creature on the pillow that had been looking back at me . . . OMG . . . I had no clue what obviously had been preparing to sneak up and attack me. My heart was racing. I'm sure I looked like the commercial of the startled kitten clinging to the ceiling because that's exactly how I felt at that moment. I'm fearless when anyone or anything does something to jeopardize the success of one of my programs—man or beast. I'm ready to take them on. My own inner convictions, past experiences and my co-worker Yul's defense training has prepared me for most anything. Insects and creepy crawlers, however, make me go all girly. While I love to be in nature, I don't want nature to be physically *on* me, especially species I can't identify.

Time to find out what my present tiny terror attacker was. Lizards or tree frogs in my room I can handle, but while this new species was green, it was neither of those two and its huge eyes were watching my every move as closely as I was watching its. No way would I feel comfortable in my suite until my tiny menace was captured and carefully removed. I breathed a sigh of relief when housekeeping took my capture away with a respectful snicker and dutifully noted the tip on my expense report: Expense account entry: Tipping $10.00 for the removal of one extra large praying mantis. The rest of my stay in Mauritius was uneventful. My driver was wonderful. The venues we selected for group functions were perfect and tomorrow it will be time to reboard the plane and head for the Seychelles, but this time I'm rested, refreshed and ready to travel the world again.

SEPTEMBER 23

I had always heard that the Seychelles had some of the most beautiful beaches in the world and I certainly wasn't disappointed. Watching the incredible sunset made me long to be sharing the experience with someone special in my life. I could now understand why many company owners flew their partners in pre or post program and extended their stay so they could share the wonder of what they were seeing and experiencing with someone they loved. Together they made work play and play work. Maybe someday I would go down that path again but with the partner and playmate I was meant to be with. I would leave that in the hands of God/the universe. Right now my only plans include an early night.

Tomorrow I'm going to play tourist. No schedules, no private cars and drivers—just me, myself and about 20 other people taking a boat trip to a small island that the resort's activity director had recommended. I haven't done something like that in years and just want to experience a day where I haven't been wined, dined or wooed for my business.

SEPTEMBER 24

The trip started out pleasantly enough. A couple of families, honeymooners, two retired gentlemen traveling the world and me. It was great to be on the water enjoying the sunshine on my face, the breeze in my hair and the happy voices around me. We were off to spend the day at a private island. The host—an author and the owner of the island—would be letting us enjoy his world for the day. The beach was ours to enjoy, hammocks were set up to relax and read in, a walking tour of the island could be arranged and a casual luncheon would be served midday. The boat dropped us off and then left, the staff saying they would be back at 3 to pick us up. That surprised me, as I am used to having transportation waiting on standby in case of emergencies or plans changing. But no one else seemed particularly concerned. They found their place in the sun and settled in to enjoy the feeling of having their own private island retreat for the day.

The host came out to greet us and welcome everyone to his island and started to run through what we needed to know about the amenities, facilities and the like available to us. Suddenly the quiet was shattered by the frantic barking of his dogs and the host went to quiet them down. We heard a loud noise and in a few minutes the host reappeared seeming shaken and with blood oozing from a gash on his forehead. He said an intruder was on the island looking to steal our purses, cameras, etc. and that he had battled with him and been overpowered. The host and his staff had radioed for the police to come and also to find out if anyone had escaped from the prison that was set up on a nearby island. It apparently was swimming distance away and the host feared that if it was not just robbers that had come onto the island, it was someone planning to pick up an escaped convict. The host was off with his staff and dogs to check the other side of the island to see if he could find the intruder's (or was it intruders'???) boat and stop them from leaving. We could either stay and wait on our own for them to return or we could come with them. Where is Yul when you need him?

Everyone opted not to be left on his or her own and we began our adventure around the island, each one helping the next slide down slopes and climb over branches and rocks. It felt like a scene from *Lost* and we didn't know who or what we were searching for. We discovered the boat the intruders had used to get to our island and the host's staff rendered it unusable for escape. Now we had intruders—and maybe escaped convicts—trapped on the island with no means of leaving, which was the exact same position we were in. Hot, tired, sweaty, bitten by bugs and scratched, we made our way back to the main house after traversing the entire island and finding no sign of the intruders. From time to time the dogs would bark, but nothing like this morning. By the time we got back, the police boat had arrived to check on us and let us know our boat would be making its way back to us. The police were now heading over to the prison to check and make sure all was in order over there. They offered to leave an officer with us for protection but the host said we should be okay and that we would be staying put. We took turns showering in the open-air shower, tended to our cuts and bruises and sat down to eat lunch. Everyone was on edge and the slightest noise made us jump. Adrenaline was pumping through everyone. When our boat reappeared, we all gratefully made our good-byes, wishing the host well. Everyone on board was all wound up and couldn't stop talking about their encounter.

Having crafted murder mysteries and the like for special events, my imagination was working overtime. Was it real or was it illusion? I'll never tell. Tricks of the trade and all that. This experience

gave insight as to what clients experience when we include unexpected—but carefully planned—surprises for them. I could see
how some could cause anxiety and others anticipation. Another
thing I knew was that at the end of the day I'd be very ready to go
back to being a pampered princess, do room service and relax in a
bathtub built for two, filled with fragrant bubbles, and be fresh for
tomorrow when my formal fam trip activities began.

SEPTEMBER 30

Done. Done. Done. Ready to fly home tomorrow. I feel I've ex-
plored every inch of the Seychelles and now know it inside out,
which was the purpose of my stay.

Do a full tour of the island. Check.

See every resort that we would consider using and do a full
site inspection of the property. Check.

Look at off-property venues with local DMC and discuss theme
possibilities. Check.

Experience dining in the restaurants we would use for dine-
around programs and private takeovers. Check.

Sample the nightlife and select the best options for our program guests. Check.

Review all land, air and sea activities we can create for our
event. Check.

Take lots of pictures and notes in order to do full presentation
to staff when I get back and have the material I need on hand to
prepare client proposals. Check.

My site of Mauritius was much less intense. As it was a site
inspection and I was familiar with the destination, I only had to
check out the actual resort and venues we would be using on this
proposed program and a few new event elements that had come
into being since our last trip here like new resorts, restaurants, etc.
A site inspection is essentially a dry run of your event program and

a chance to see if all the event elements are still up to par and will deliver the results that you are looking for. Seychelles was different as it was a true fam and no one from the company had been there before, and it was important to maximize being there and see as much as possible and assess what would be a fit for different clients and different budgets. Really, wish I had both the time and the energy to check out the Maldives while I was in this part of the world, but I'll have to make that trip another time. The Maldives is one place I would love to see both personally and professionally. That's one of the perks of the business—when personal pursuits are work and work is play.

LONG COMMUTE TO WORK: Q&A

Site Inspections

Q: Who should go on site inspections?

A: It can vary from site inspection to site inspection. A sales rep may go with the event designer, event operations staff, a senior member of executive staff, a trusted freelance event/trip director with the client or client's representatives or, as in this example, on their own. Whether you're traveling on your own or with your client, personal safety is always a factor. Site inspections are arranged through the hotel you are considering contracting and with the DMC as well. The hotel will be responsible for making sure that you (and your clients) experience all the resort facilities, from their spa to their top dining rooms. They will take you on a tour of the property and show you the various room types and a selection of suites. You'll be able to see your function space during the day and by night.

The DMC, and sometimes the tourist board, will handle the rest of your stay. At times they will accompany you, and at others they will send you out with a personal driver who will be following the detailed itinerary you have worked out with your DMC. Your local tourist board can advise you on the areas to see and which to avoid. Having a personal driver assigned to you is recommended always. That way you are not driving on unfamiliar roads and spending energy and time looking for parking spaces, you can leave things in the car and have greater personal safety, etc.

If the client has opted to have the event planning staff conduct the site inspection on their own, on their behalf, it is advisable to send out senior company representatives that are

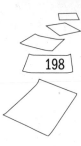

experienced in knowing what will or will not meet both your company standards and the client's event criteria. They will be signing off, accepting your recommended selections, through contracts, which may need to be amended post site inspection visit. If the client chooses not to go or send a company representation, it will be important to provide a full report—with pictures, etc.—to the client upon your return.

Assignment

Discuss the reasons it would be beneficial to have the event designer or event operations staff accompany the sales representatives on their site inspection, the value it could bring to successfully executing the event and other pluses.

Site Inspection vs. Fam Trip

Q: What is the difference between a site inspection and a familiarization trip?

A: A site inspection is a trip that is tied to a specific event program, taken to review the event inclusions and venues and to move the program to contract. The cost for the site inspection is included in the event cost for "x" number of event planning representatives and "x" number of client representatives. A familiarization trip is a hosted trip put on by a tourist board and/or a combination of airlines, hotels, ground operators, cruise ships, venues, event industry services, etc. It is designed to showcase the caliber of service, etc. that would be provided, a destination, or a resort to build working relationships and result in new business. Sometimes there is a minimum fee charged to take part in a familiarization trip and other times there is no fee attached. Sometimes a familiarization trip can be arranged for an individual.

Assignment

Discuss the value of familiarization trips to event planners, event planning companies, their clients and to the suppliers.

Site Inspection and Fam Trip Protocol

Q: Do site inspections and familiarization trips get abused?

A: There is abuse of the system. Sometimes clients are given, as a booking perk, site inspections in destinations that have personal interest but to which they have no intention of ever booking a group or event. The same happens with regard to familiarization trips when they are used as a personal vacation or even given to—in the case of one event planning company—an owner's parents who were not working for the event planning company but had a desire to travel to a specific location and extend their trip there for their personal vacation, saving the cost of airfare, and requesting special rates at the hotel for their post familiarization stay. Event planning companies are not always aware that their employees have approached or accepted familiarization trips to be used as a personal perk and a cheap vacation until they hear about it later from the supplier looking for business from the company in return.

Assignment

Discuss policies that event planning companies could put into place to stop site inspection and familiarization trip abuse, and the reasons why it is important not to accept them unless it is truly a destination, resort, etc. that the company intends to use.

Checking Out the Competition

Q: When you are on a site inspection or familiarization trip, is it okay to look at other hotel properties, set up meetings with other suppliers and see different venues?

A: Each familiarization trip is set up differently. Some familiarization trips do not leave you a minute to breathe, as they have been set up such that there will be no free time to explore other options—but event planners have been known to visit other properties in the wee hours of the morning if they have no time during the day and they are equally determined to see them. Other familiarization trips build in free time to allow planners to do so, knowing they will visit them anyhow; they are confident enough in what they are offering that they are unconcerned. They believe that event planners seeing the competition will actually work in their favor. And they also want event planners to have time to investigate options that may be right for their clients but not necessarily the entire group. For example, taking advantage of the opportunity to try hot air ballooning to learn the event logistics firsthand in a destination that offers that, if it is something that no one in the office has previous experience with and you do have the clients with the budgets to be able to afford that type of activity on a program. One event planner discovered a white chocolate fountain made from a glass slipper and party favors—a cookie shaped into a star on a "magic wand"—that sparked a Cinderella theme event that was perfect for their client traveling to the destination and something they could use elsewhere, shipping them in, for another future event where a star cookie on a stick would be a fitting centerpiece addition.

A site inspection is different, especially if you are traveling with a client. The intent of a site inspection is to finalize the event program and let the client experience the destination, the resort and the actual program. Many clients prefer a relaxed pace—making the site inspection into a mini-vacation—especially if they have brought their spouse along, which frequently happens. They are not looking to be dragged around looking at other hotels unless they are still deciding between two presented. If the event planner needs to check out other options for other companies for the future or look at new venues, etc., they can either schedule free time for the client to relax and enjoy the resort or fly in earlier or stay on longer than the client. In the case of the event planner arriving earlier or staying later, many times the sales rep will be the one flying with the client to make sure that their trip to and from the destination is stress free. It is generally a good idea to cost in two event planning representatives to go on a site inspection, with one person advancing—as would happen on the client's program—and the sales rep staying with the client.

Assignment
Discuss what would be important to see and do on a familiarization trip.

Expected Codes of Conduct on Fam Trips and Site Inspections

Q: How is expected behavior on a familiarization trip different than expected behavior on a site inspection?

A: In both cases, it should never be forgotten that you are there as a professional and as a representative of your company. Showing up dressed inappropriately, drinking, not being on time, etc.

is not acceptable behavior on either a familiarization trip or site inspection. It is important to remember that while the setting may be more relaxed being at a resort than in a boardroom, business is still being conducted.

Assignment

Name five company codes of conduct that you feel would be important to adhere to on a familiarization trip and/or site inspection.

Supplier Expectations

Q: Other than return business, is there anything else that suppliers will be looking for from event planning companies and their staff who have taken part in a familiarization trip and/or site inspection?

A: Familiarization trip and site inspection hosts will be looking for access to you and company employees when they are calling to set up sales calls. Bring around the other hotel or suppliers they represent, see support by full office attendance at their supplier events and presentations, etc. Some suppliers say they feel used and abused when they receive not as much as a thank-you note and are turned down repeatedly—if their call or e-mail is even returned—when they try to set up a sales meeting.

Assignment

Discuss what company qualifications would be important to be met in order for a company employee to accept an invitation for a familiarization trip or ask for special personal vacation concessions from suppliers.

Maximizing the Value of Fam Trips and Site Inspections

Q: Beyond a thank-you note, is there anything else that should be done post familiarization trip and/or site inspection?

A: In furthering the educational value of familiarization trips and site inspections, successful event planning companies use them as a means of in-house training, hold post travel meetings to review the findings, and require a full written report to be made for their company resource and reference files.

Assignment

Design a sample familiarization trip/site inspection questionnaire that would provide great feedback as a training tool for others in the office.

Expense Reports

Q: What is an expense report?

A: An expense report captures all charges that take place during a familiarization trip and/or site inspection. If it's for a site inspection, some expenses may be charged back to the file and others may be deemed an office expense. Backup is usually required. Expense reports are also used on-site when the event is running, as well. Some companies, instead of having staff report meals on their expense reports, simply give a meal allowance, appropriate for the resort that the staff is staying at, to cover three meals a day, taxes, tipping, etc. Should the staff member exceed the amount, they are responsible for the difference. If they prefer to eat light, the additional funds are theirs to keep. Each event planning company has different policies and procedures in place. Some companies have staff sign all

meals to the master account but do put guidelines in place re-garding dollar amount, what type of drinks will be covered, etc.

Assignment

Discuss the merits of different ways of handling expenses relating to meals and what should and should not be a covered expense on site inspections, familiarization trips and the program.

Drawing the Line on Event "Surprises"

Q: When designing an event with unexpected twists and turns, how far is too far to go?

A: You need to keep the audience in mind and how what you are proposing is being presented. A mock motor coach "holdup," for example, created real alarm for guests en route to an evening function, as they did not know it was a planned event. The idea was to capture top salespeople and then do a sales shootout. That event element backfired. One event planning company had their motor coach stop to pick up a scary looking hitchhiker by the road, who happened to be a surprise entertainment feature to make the long trip more fun. As he immediately began to play and entertain the guests, they immediately knew that he was a planned part of their entertainment. The event planners' calm response to the hitchhiker boarding was a tip-off that this was scheduled. You need to look carefully at how, when, what and where to throw in anything that could cause guest anxiety instead of anticipation, and always do so with full client sign-off and approval.

Assignment

Give some examples of event planning "surprises" that could initially raise guest alarm.

CHAPTER

9 GUESTS GONE WILD

Em and her team have to deal with an abusive guest who goes out of control, is fired on the spot and is sent back home but not before causing more havoc and added drama. The order of the day was to juggle dealing with the guest's removal and operating the program so that the rest of the guests were not privy to what was taking place behind the scenes. It was up to Em and her staff to pull this off, restore order, instill a feeling of calm and bring their event back on track in order to achieve the desired event results.

OCTOBER 16

I will never forget the sound of his voice. "If I can't speak to her I am going to kill myself," said the voice on the phone. He still sounded high on something that wasn't the Mexican beer and margaritas we'd served at the final check-in point for today's team-building challenge that had them ending up at the beach for a private party. Would this day or week ever come to an end???

The morning had started out peacefully enough. Beautiful blue skies, balmy sunny weather, guests in high spirits setting out with their experienced—in the goings-on of corporate antics—Mexican drivers for a day of corporate play where the goal was to

produce one-minute company commercials for a new product that was about to be launched.

Having learned our lesson with the laundromat escapades from the earlier program involving a sales force with an equally competitive nature, PG was the rating given for these company productions. We wanted to make sure that none of the acts caught on film today were suggestive or crossed the line and ventured into "sex tapes" territory. Given the nature of some of the goods their company manufactured, it was a distinct possibility that I would not put past some of their winners.

Couples were divided into teams and got to choose the role they wanted to take on. Outgoing or shy, there was something for everyone and they could take on dual roles as well. Each team selected someone to be the director, scriptwriter, camera operator, actor, grip, stylist and makeup artist. Armed with a video camera, recording tape and batteries, each team set out with their driver to film their masterpiece. Their drivers were at their disposal to help them scout suitable locations for filming, be on hand to offer whatever assistance they required and bring them to the check-in beach party for an afternoon of relaxation and sharing the experiences of the day—without giving too much away—over a drink or two before returning to the resort. The plan for tomorrow was for them to continue the process of bonding as a team and work closely with a professional video editing team to add the finishing touches to their film production, adding background music, text and special effects.

Today was about coming together as a team creatively, and tomorrow will be about team collaboration. The other team-building challenges we had considered were building a boat and having a float-your-boat race, and a version of corporate geocaching using a handheld GPS system to find hidden clues that would tie into the new product, but the corporate execs loved the idea of seeing what their top sales team collectively could come up with to help sell their product. At their farewell theme dinner a giant screen will be set up for all to view their finished productions and awards will be handed out.

The party was ready to begin when they arrived. Great food. Great music. Great setting. One by one the "studio" cars rolled in, all except one. And not surprising it was driving the same disruptive couple that went missing early this week: MrArrogance, a self-proclaimed industry sales leader who was more feared for his explosive temper when crossed than followed by others aspiring to be him or please him at work, and his fiancée. From what we could see from the fiancée's behavior, and the troubling, dark bruises that she attributed to her being klutzy, MrArrogance had an explosive temper at home as well. MrArrogance had already turned a morning deep sea fishing excursion into a late night return. Our local DMCs were frantically trying to locate their missing boat and couldn't imagine that the boat's captain would have allowed anyone to steer him off course and not return the group at the appointed time. A search party was sent out, as contact could not be raised over their radio and it was well after dark when the lost were found. They had bribed the captain to take them to a fishing area that MrArrogance thought was better and had separated from the rest of the deep sea fishing fleet we had hired for the day. MrArrogance returned boasting about his near record-breaking catch that he was having stuffed, mounted and sent back home while his fiancée apologized profusely to his employers and fellow colleagues for the worry and concern that his actions had caused, and for having the captain head out with just the two of them aboard when MrArrogance got tired of waiting to see if the others who had signed up were still planning on coming. J.T. had just turned his back for a minute while using the telephone at the resort's beachside restaurant to check on the status of those who had not yet arrived when MrArrogance saw his chance and had the captain set off before J.T. caught sight of what he was up to.

Yul and Marco had been so busy checking in and settling their own assigned teams, making sure that safety procedures were being followed and life jackets worn, that they had not noticed what was taking place until it was too late. Everyone thought they were just getting a jump start on securing a good spot at the chosen fishing location and not bent on losing everyone as fast as they could so that they could head off in another direction.

It appeared it was time to send out another search car, as once again no contact could be made via cell phone or radio. This time not just MrArrogance and his fiancée were missing but also his "film crew" team.

MrArrogance and his fiancée (apologizing again for his boorish behavior) finally rolled in with the others who had been misled by MrArrogance. He had told them that plans had changed and the check-in lunch had been moved to dinner back at the resort to allow teams more time to film.

Something about MrArrogance's behavior was off. We were quietly discussing the possibility among ourselves that he might be on illegal drugs or had not taken required medication that day. We were moving into crisis mode management to quietly have MrArrogance removed from the scene until he could calm down. But before we could do that MrArrogance's mood quickly shifted from being a danger to himself—personally and professionally— to becoming openly belligerent, defiant and right up in the faces of the senior executives. His stance was threatening as he leaned in closer to one top exec who was standing with his back to a plate glass window. The venue's security guards started to move closer to be on hand should a need arise, but before they could get close enough to be able to react, MrArrogance raised his hand and prepared to swing hard at the company ex. Several of the company's sales team who were nearer saw what was about to take place and tackled their colleague to the ground mid swing. Had MrArrogance connected he would have sent the individual flying into, or perhaps even through, the glass window. MrArrogance was fired on the spot by company execs and led off the scene by the security team, with Yul, Marco and J.T. following. Dee Dee and Daniela went to meet with company heads to see their proposed plan of action (no matter what had taken place no one wanted MrArrogance locked up in a Mexican jail), Myki went to the side of the fiancée and took her to a private spot to help her calm down, and Vero, Jae and Lainy skillfully took care of the other guests and got the celebration back on track. I, along with one of the higher-up company executives, was on the telephone to company lawyers—both the clients and ours—seeing what needed to be done from a legal standpoint to protect everyone, and then on the telephone with the hotel and airlines. The hotel's security team packed MrArrogance's bags and he was checked out of his room. Alternate accommodation was found for him at another hotel and local DMC staff arranged to have him checked in and his bags brought there. His fiancée (or soon to be ex-fiancée) elected not to go with him and was moved to another guestroom in the hotel for her safety. Turned out to no one's surprise that the bruises she was sporting didn't come from being clumsy—that was just a cover—and yes, MrArrogance had obtained and taken drugs today. Her new room was located on the concierge floor, which had its own elevator and required a special key, and had staff stationed there 24 hours a day to be of service only to guests staying on these floors. As well, her name was taken off of the hotel's guest list so that incoming calls would not be directed to her. Hotel security was apprised of the situation and were already aware of who MrArrogance was from previous run-ins during his stay. Apparently, they'd been called to his room several times last night because of hotel guests' complaints about loud screaming and voices coming from their room, but hadn't let anyone on my staff know about that as yet as we'd been up and out of the hotel early today.

MrArrogance was not to be permitted back on the hotel grounds and would be sent home tomorrow. His plane tickets had been changed and he was no longer flying home with the group. There were no direct flights back the next morning so MrArrogance would be connecting on his return in a city as far as possible from here so that he could not double back and drive in from a closer connecting city. It was also noted on his file that he was not allowed to change his tickets to an alternate route or receive a refund. Someone from security would be escorting MrArrogance to the airport tomorrow, turning him over to airport security and, as a safeguard, staying at the airport until the plane departed to make sure that he was on it.

Then the calls started to come in. MrArrogance, after being driven to his new hotel, had tried to return, had been turned away and, thwarted, started a call-in campaign to try and reach his fiancée, which he couldn't. She didn't want to talk to him and was under the protective care of his ex-company and some of the wives of the senior execs. He also couldn't reach any of the company heads or fellow guests, as the operators could now recognize his voice and were under instructions not to put him through to them. I was next on his list, and the calls coming in threatening suicide began, telling us that we would have to ship his body home. Daniela dryly remarked that it would be easier to deal with than this, as she knew the procedures for shipping and handling of goods out of the country to be sent to his home; she'd already taken care of making all the arrangements for his prized catch to be safely delivered there. MrArrogance had tested her patience around that and was testing it again now. And mine.

At one point I had just hung up the telephone in the hotel lobby from speaking with him to find him on his knees begging me to let him back into the hotel, but that wasn't my decision to make. Hotel security did not understand how he had managed to slip by them and escorted him back off of the grounds, and we moved out of the public areas to prevent another scene that would only serve to upset their hotel guests. We met with the hotel execs and they were firm on their actions. There would be no reprieve for their ex-employee and they would not be hiring him back. His fiancée, however, had a change of heart and asked to be moved over to his hotel with him and elected to fly home with him. We made the arrangements for them to be reunited. After all, there's nothing we or her fiancé's ex-company could do to have her stay against her will. Stats say that it can take someone in an abusive relationship eight times before they finally leave for good.

Security said that when they dropped the fiancée off, MrArrogance seemed to be calmer. He must have been coming down from whatever he had taken. They said that when they left MrArrogance and his fiancée at the other hotel, his fiancée appeared to be in no immediate danger. Maybe this will be the wake-up call they both need and if not for both, then just his fiancée, as it's not too late to call off the wedding and reclaim a life lived without fear.

OCTOBER 17

Our responsibility today was to the guests at hand and to bringing our client's program back on track. You cannot let one bad experience mar the rest of the program. It had to go on as planned and it was our job to bring back the feeling of well-being.

The atmosphere was much lighter after MrArrogance's departure. Concern was expressed initially about the welfare of his intended, but there was nothing anyone could do. Returning with him had been her decision. And, as masters of discretion, there was nothing we could comment on about this matter even when pressed. It was up to us to lead by example and demonstrate the art of discretion so that this one event did not undo the good of their winning getaway and turn the hotel into a giant watercooler, with everyone discussing to death what had taken place.

A private group breakfast was quickly arranged and the company executives expressed what their lawyers had instructed them to say and said that at that point the matter was to be dropped and everyone was to move forward with the day's agenda. Luckily MrArrogance and his fiancée had played behind-the-scenes roles in yesterday's filming, so the rest of their team could still take part in putting the finishing touches on their day's endeavor.

OCTOBER 20

The rest of the week passed without further incident and the results from the day of filming were surprisingly good—so good, in fact, that the company is going to use some of the ideas in their upcoming campaign and the winning teams are going to get the chance to be part of shooting an actual commercial!

You can plan and prepare but you never know exactly how an event will unfold. Expecting the unexpected to happen is the best you can do. Anticipate, have a backup plan and know what to do when crisis strikes, and I've learned that applies equally in life as in event production. You can predict to a point the human element and how people interact with one another, but you have to be ready to handle twists and turns along the way. Some can be sad, as in the death of a beloved guest; serious, as in this case; or heartwarming, as in the case of one couple (both company employees and both top sales winners) on the trip, who with Daniela's and Marco's on-site help and the prior approval of their company execs, invited all guests on a day that was marked as "at leisure" to their destination wedding, which they had been keeping a secret. This event, unplanned by us, helped to push MrArrogance totally out of the minds of all the rest of the guests. Had we not known this was taking place, we would've suggested doing something fueled by great emotional energy that would have delivered the same results to get our event back on track. Having a wedding take place in the middle of this program was just what we needed!

Customized wedding invitations hand-painted by the resort's local artists on a Mexican tile base slipped inside a leather envelope with the bride and groom's engraved initials were delivered to each guestroom the night before the wedding was scheduled to take place. They were beautifully done up but had to be redone before they could be delivered—Myki discovered the pink ribbon (part of the couple's color scheme) used on the small miniature bouquets that were to accompany them bore a message imprinted on the ribbon proudly proclaiming, "It's a girl." Um. Wasn't true. And not the message you necessarily want to send out accompanying your wedding invitation, even if it were. Talk about watercooler fodder!

Guests were delighted to be asked to attend their sunset wedding celebration. Tiki torches and candles lined the pathway to their ceremony and reception dinner location. Their wedding ceremony took place under a wooden pavilion draped with white curtains. A private lounge area had been set up on a romantic section of the resort's beach and the couple had arranged for their wedding guests to enjoy a grilled buffet dinner and cocktails as the sun set into the ocean after their ceremony. Guests dined on local specialties, such as lobster, turkey with "mole de rancho" sauce, prawns, Mexican rice, frijoles puercos (beans mixed with pork, sausages) and a tres leches ("three milks") wedding cake with tequila. Mango, lemon, strawberry and tamarindo margaritas and icy Mexican beers were also served. A mariachi band provided background music during cocktails and a high-energy band played for the rest of the night and had the wedding guests up and dancing barefoot on the beach under a sky filled with twinkling stars that cast streaks of silver across turquoise water.

OCTOBER 22

Despite its beginning, the program ended on a high note, with the wedding an added bonus for watercooler talk back in the office instead of the focus being on MrArrogance being fired. He's already a distant memory in the minds of the participants and his office has been cleaned out, and his replacement already has been installed.

The farewell evening was spectacular. I was really happy with how we turned our program around and glad we had a couple of days after the upsetting incident to put it out of the participants' minds, but I also know that even without the couple of days we still would have been able to turn it all around.

GUESTS GONE WILD: Q&A

Legal Responsibilities and Legal Repercussions

Q: If the client's employees or venue security had not been close enough to stop a dangerous situation from escalating, would the event planning staff have been required to step in and stop him from striking the company executive?

A: To have a clear course of action to follow when violence occurs, discuss this type of issue in advance with company lawyers. Questions need to be answered, such as could event planning staff be charged by the aggressor for putting their hands on them, especially if they had been injured in the takedown? What would the legal repercussions be personally and to the company? Would the recommended action be to step back and get security to handle the matter?

Assignment

Not all security companies are created equal. One event planning company makes it a company policy that where they deem additional security to be necessary they only hire off-duty police officers who know the law, know what to do and how to do it as opposed to a security company that may have no formal training in this area. Discuss other measures event planning companies can take to protect themselves, their staff, their suppliers, their client and other guests.

Removing a Guest from an Event

Q: Did the event planning company and client have the right to move MrArrogance out of his hotel room to another hotel?

A: In this case, the client, not MrArrogance, had booked and paid for the guestroom. Had the person causing the disruption been paying for his room on his own, which can happen, e.g., if attending a conference, the hotel—not the client—would have had to make that call. Along with knowing your company's position on guest safety and security, you also need to review with your suppliers their crisis management plans before your event takes place and you need to know what you can and cannot do. For example, if the hotel had requested that event planning staff pack MrArrogance's bags, is this something that they should be doing or legally should the hotel be handling it?

Assignment

Name and discuss key areas of guest safety and security that need to be addressed pre program.

Client Responsibility

Q: Did the company have the right to force the individual to fly home the next day?

A: The company was picking up the cost of the single night in the other hotel and the return ticket home. The company executives informed MrArrogance that if he did not comply with the request, he would be responsible for making his own way home. Again, this is an area that needs to be discussed with company lawyers and staff safety needs to be addressed as well. For example, should an event planning staff member be requested to see the individual off at the airport? If so, should they bring security with them or have security bring the individual to the airport?

Company Lawyers

Q: Is there anything special that needs to be done when something like this takes place?

A: Company lawyers of all involved parties will have certain requirements that they will want to see put into place, e.g., official written documentation of what took place, signatures on witness statements, etc. It is essential for event planning companies to have company policies, procedures and protocols in place that have been sanctioned by company lawyers and to make sure that they are reviewed and signed off by staff members. You need to have a crisis management plan in place so that your staff know what they can do and when they need to bring in help. Someone on program should also have the emergency number to reach the company lawyer should something unexpected happen.

Witnessing Illegal Activities

Q: What course of action should be taken if an event planning staff member sees or hears about drug use taking place or sees someone with a concealed weapon at their event?

A: Again, this is an area that needs to have prior in-office discussion and legal advice on steps that need to be taken. For example, should the client be informed before taking a prescribed course of action?

Assignment

Discuss various ways that event planning companies can be proactive to stop or limit drug use at one of their events. (Answer: hiring bathroom attendants, hiring off-duty police as security, etc.)

Abusive Guests

Q: If signs of spousal abuse or any other type of abuse are identified, are event planning staff required to step in?

A: This is an area that could be and should be discussed with company lawyers. Partner and spousal abuse—physical and verbal—can take place whether or not drinking is involved. Some participants simply make the mistake of bringing guests that they do not know well to company/business events. Planners are skilled at defusing heated moments that sometimes can occur during an event, but when things escalate, it's imperative that staff know how they are to handle specific dangerous situations.

Assignment
Identify what type of scenario would be considered a heated moment as opposed to an act of physical and verbal abuse.

Handling Emergency Situations

Q: Should any other action have been taken when MrArrogance was threatening suicide as opposed to just moving him to another hotel and leaving him on his own for the night in a poor state of mind?

A: Each event brings learning lessons. As you learn and grow, you'll discover new issues that will need to be reviewed with legal counsel and be added to company policy and procedures. Make an emergency call for legal direction as soon as an unfamiliar situation arises, and be sure to discuss your findings in a post event meeting so that all staff are informed as to an appropriate course of legal action.

Assignment
Discuss other key emergency situation areas that should be covered and clear directions that should be given to event planning staff.

Guests Gone Missing

Q: How could the fishing boat incident have been handled so that the guest was not able to take control of the boat?

A: Well, by having ground rules in place and reviewed with the captain of each boat as to whose requests they are to respond to. Having a staff member—local DMC staff or event planning

staff—physically onboard each boat would have ensured the boat's whereabouts were known.

Assignment

Name other types of events where guests go off in teams or individuals where you would need to put safety measures in place. One example is in an earlier chapter. (Answer: building in checkpoint stops on a car rally to keep close tabs on the cars. Another one is having a chase car to follow the hot air balloons.)

CHAPTER

10 TAKING AN ETHICAL STAND

Em has to make the decision whether to keep or "fire" a client. She has her personal and company's reputation at stake and knows that it is best to walk away from business that is not aligned with your company standards and ethical beliefs.

NOVEMBER 4

We've had the privilege of working with some wonderful clients. And, we've had our share of clients that just make you shake your head, knowing that they're setting themselves up for getting caught one day with their hand in their company's financial cookie jar.

For one particular company, we did a six-week back-to-back program in a luxury resort. Each week the program repeated. Their incentive program was so successful that they outgrew the space they had on hold and the only recourse was to run back-to-back groups or move the dates to another time, which the client—the company president—did not want to do as what was originally a company event turned into a summer holiday for his four children and their nanny. The kids and nanny had their own suites and full run of the hotel and the company's master expense account. Their nanny exercised very little control over the kids, as she was far too busy looking for a possible future husband to take her away from her babysitting fate.

When the company pres received the total bill for his children's six-plus-weeks-long free-for-all added to the cost to have his family housed in the resort's top suites, he was stunned to see an amount close to six figures. He had been warned by Dee Dee that it was climbing excessively high but dismissed it with a wave of his hand every time she tried to make him aware of what was taking place. He simply signed off on all the bills presented to him, telling Dee Dee that he did not have time to deal with that and everything his children and their nanny wanted had his approval. Then it was our turn to be stunned when the resort's sales rep came to us telling us that our client wanted those charges to disappear from the resort's books and be distributed as fictitious ballroom rental charges so that they could be put through the company's books and paid without becoming a red flag. The resort was happy to comply with the client's request—they received many such creative costing demands—but wanted us to be aware of what was taking place so that we did not question the charges as the resort was presenting them. Reviewing and doing the final reconciliations falls under what we normally do, but it is one service that this particular client did not want us to provide. He wanted his personal executive assistant to handle the reconciliation, which is why he wanted to sign the hotel contract directly—which is not the norm—and which is why he had no problem going directly to the resort to make his request. Now we understood the reason why. We would have questioned the charges and his personal executive assistant, who had brought her spouse along on the trip for the six weeks.

We found ourselves in one of those put-your-cards-on-the-table-and-be-prepared-to-walk-away moments and that's exactly what we did. Our services officially ended once everyone was on their way home and we had fulfilled all of our contractual duties. The final reconciliation and how the client chose to handle his personal accounting was now between him and the resort. It was not surprising soon after to read in the newspapers that their company went out of business. Apparently, there were a lot of hands in that company cookie jar. There is a *big* difference between being a master of discretion and being a master of deception. Oh, and the nanny? It turned out to be a very financially advantageous six-week vacation for her, as she became wife number five—or was it six—of one of the top producers on the trip (we'd seen so many come and go it was easy to lose track).

It is important to lead by example and I was proud of how my taking a stand with a client was embraced and supported by my staff. It's hard walking away from half-a-million-dollar accounts, but it's also hard living with yourself if you compromise your ethics. In life you have to choose carefully whom you want to partner with and get into bed with. When you are in a committed relationship, be it personal or business, giving your all to make your partnership a success, you have to think about how your actions will be perceived and how they will affect others. There are two entities involved. Ideally you want to align yourself with someone whose core personal values and work ethics are the same as yours.

And my actions led Jake to take action with one of his clients. Jake had been working hard to land an account that was worth a lot of money to both him and our company—this one was well over $750,000—and was very close to sealing the deal, but when the time came, he couldn't. In his meetings with his client, many after hours in his office over a drink, he had the chance to observe his client's business practices and what he saw and heard left an impression.

While talking to Jake the client would make the office rounds and go through employees' personal effects and letters. Nothing was sacred. Although one employee must have noticed something different with her desk when she came in in the morning, as she had made a note in her daybook to talk to her manager about someone going through her things.

The client apparently had an ear for music and had memorized his staff's personal telephone passwords, which he was able to

CHAPTER TEN

decipher from the notes played when they punched in their codes, and took great glee in playing one of his married sales staff's messages from his mistress.

The client often put people calling in on speakerphone when Jake was in the room, motioning him to be quiet and listen in without letting the other party know that someone else was in the room listening to what they thought was a private conversation.

What none of his staff members, clients and suppliers knew was that in the client's briefcase resting open on his filing cabinet was a hidden microphone he used to tape conversations. One day he had proudly showed it to Jake, leading Jake to wonder how many of his conversations had been taped and shared with others without his knowledge.

Jake also knew that when his executives were in closed-door meetings with their employees the client listened in to their private talks by using his telephone's intercom system. Unless the exec noticed the red light on, they had no idea that their meeting was being monitored. Jake did because, for whatever reason—maybe his client thought he had a partner in crime with Jake—he openly did that in front of him. Jake was appalled. And Jake was not pulled into his client's teary sob stories about how much he missed his children (he was recently divorced and remarried). Pulling out their pictures to show others what a caring and feeling dad he was, was just an act. Jake had witnessed huge battles where neither parent wanted their kids for the weekend. Their kids were totally messed up and it was easy to see why.

Appearances were everything to the client and it was more important to the client to drive a brand new expensive car every year, have golf and country club memberships that ran in the six figures and to give his new wife carte blanche to renovate their home as many times as her heart desired than to make sure that his office staff, whom Jake had seen struggling to get their jobs done, had the right equipment.

Jake also saw the client take great pleasure in ripping his own customers off and taking profits that did not belong to him and also knew from careful observance that the client thought that his employees' work was beneath him. In crunch situations he would rather hire someone to stuff an envelope than roll up his sleeves and jump in to do what needed to be done. Or he'd slip out the back door to his office to escape while they worked late into the night without compensation.

The client also boasted of how he was deliberately working his sales reps' customers behind their backs, setting up meetings with them when his sales reps were out of town or on vacation and sometimes even in front of them. He would invite their clients to spend the weekend with him and his wife and cut the sales rep out of taking part to ensure personal loyalty to him, not the sales rep, should the rep ever decide to leave.

The client also revealed to Jake how he worked the sales reps' figures in his favor so that they did not receive all the monies due to them, and said if they were unhappy they could leave—which was better for him because if they left their clients stayed and they would receive no further revenue.

This client took family members and friends along on his trips and billed the expenses back to the company, listing them as customers.

This client was on the take whenever and however he could and he made it clear to Jake that in return for business he expected free vacations, and had already provided Jake with a list of his favorite brands of liquor and wine.

Jake thought long and hard about what the client had shared with him and wondered what else he was capable of doing. In the end, Jake said—and directly to him—that the client's standards were not his and he could not do business with him. I was very proud of him. We all were.

And Jake? He found a replacement client that was the perfect match for both him and us. He experienced a yin yang moment when he met a client in the same industry as the other but with an entirely different set of principles and who radiated personal and professional integrity. Jake said the experience left him feeling like he had an "Alice in Wonderland" moment. This new client, recently divorced as well, put the well-being of his children and his employees first.

This client rented a house in the same area as his ex-wife so that his kids always had close access to their mother and would not have to be separated from their after-school friends, and felt that having them for the weekend was a privilege and a pleasure.

This client lived in a fairly empty house and drove an old car until he could afford to do otherwise, because any funds that came in during the early years were invested into the company and his employees, making sure that they had all that they needed to get through what they were hired to do. He worked side by side with his employees when a job had to get done. He stayed till the end. If he couldn't help, he could at least make coffee and ensure they took time out to eat.

This client's business grew in leaps and bounds and attracted their industry's top talent because of the respect he showed those with whom he worked and did business and everyone, including us, pulled together to give their personal and professional best back to this client and add to his company's tremendous success.

And the other client? His business limped along and never achieved anything near what his competition did, as stories of his deceptions and underhandedness came to light and swirled about in their industry. Jake heard horror stories from his peers and was grateful it wasn't him or us going through what they went through. Jake learned that becoming a master of discernment is as important as mastering the art of discretion.

TAKING AN ETHICAL STAND: Q&A

Responsibility to the Company

Q: When should employees go to their employers with clients' questionable acts?

A: As soon as possible. That will allow the event planning company to decide on an appropriate course of action that will protect their company, their employees and in many cases their client's company if the questionable actions are from a company employee as opposed to the company owner. And it's the same in reverse. One business reported a sales rep's questionable behavior to an event planning owner when in order to secure their business, the sales rep was making promises of sending the client on free fam trips that would be to destinations of his choosing for a personal vacation. In another case, a hotel reported an event planning staff member to the event planning company owner when they discovered that the employee, in charge of staying on after the group to handle the reconciliation, had invited friends down to stay with them and were charging all their expenses back to the client's master account. One freelance trip director felt that she needed to tell the event planning company owners she was working for that their sales rep had joined in an impromptu "naked pool party" at one client event they were in charge of, joining some of their client's guests. The sales rep's unprofessional antics cost the event planning company their client, as the client felt it was the responsibility of the event planning company to keep his guests under control and not join in or encourage their unprofessional shenanigans.

Assignment

Review the client behavior in the chapter and list those that would warrant action being taken and company heads being brought in to develop a course of appropriate action. What lines would have to be crossed for you to consider "firing" your client?

Ethical Behavior

Q: How can guidelines best be presented as to expected ethical behavior on the part of event planning companies, their employees, freelance staff, their suppliers and their clients?

A: Establishing a formal company policy, procedures and protocol manual that is reviewed and signed off by staff members will start the progress. And pre event meetings and post event reviews are other opportunities to open discussion on company codes of conduct.

Assignment

Make a list of areas that should be covered in a company policy, procedures and protocol manual and then create a detailed list of what needs to be addressed under each heading. For example, one area could be company dress and then under that heading would be in office, client meetings, supplier presentations, fam trips and site inspections—during business and during off time, and while on-site, during business and during off time, etc. And then do the same regarding expected codes of conducts from suppliers and clients and recommend a course of appropriate action. For example, during the recent U.S. presidential campaign, Sarah Palin reportedly came out to greet those who were conducting a business meeting with her at her hotel during the campaign dressed in a towel, with a wet towel wrapped around her head. Many event planning, client and supplier meetings take place outside the boardroom and sometimes do take place in their hotel guestrooms. If you are an event planning staff member who needed to speak with your client while on program during a stay at a resort, what would be the appropriate course of action to take if your client answered the door wrapped in a towel?

CHAPTER

11 SOCIAL AGENDA

Em and her team take on their first nonprofit event as their way to give back. After attending several charity events and seeing major missteps costing the nonprofit company tens to hundreds of thousands of dollars in fund-raising—and after receiving numerous calls to step in at the very last minute—Em concedes to take one on from the very beginning. She experiences firsthand the challenges nonprofits face when creating events with limited funds; trying to raise sponsorship dollars and awareness; and depending on their appointed chairs—patrons of their cause—to help them bring in much needed dollars, attendees, silent auction articles, publicity and volunteers to do the work and help them to run the event.

NOVEMBER 16

Dee Dee, Daniela and I felt we had been transported to an alternate event planning universe when we received a frantic phone call from a stranger who turned out to be a full-fledged, lifelong, card-carrying member of a very exclusive club, the Ladies Who Lunch a.k.a. The High Society Lunch Bunch. It was surprising for us to discover that a very select few of its members were on a mission not to better the world through their acts of good deeds but to better their social ranking by using events with a cause as a means to help them gain social status and garner good personal PR.

Some of the actions we witnessed gave us pause but also gave us some very valuable lessons in return, including a new appreciation for what nonprofit organizations face when putting together an event without dollars allocated to fund it. They have the added pressure of not only raising dollars and awareness for their cause but the dollars to run it as well. They do an amazing job, but there is a cost they can end up paying, depending on who they partnered with as their event's chairperson, as we discovered. We soon learned that there are two very different types of charity chairs. With more and more corporations partnering with nonprofits, what we took away gave us valuable insight as to what we would be facing now that many of our corporate clients wanted us to start exploring cause marketing event options that would tie their name to a charity that was a fit for them.

The events these Ladies Who Lunch—PamperedPartyPrincesses was our original pet name for them—got involved with came with a definite social agenda. When we answered their panic-stricken call to help (which we did for altruistic reasons; we viewed it as a means to give back by contributing our talents for free to what we believed was a very worthy cause) we were taken behind the scenes into a world of socialite chairs and committee members who were using chairing and heading committees for gala fund-raisers as a means to climb the social ladder and to achieve international visibility. Their personal agendas of social power, press, fashion, increasing their standing or controlling their social circles, even finding their first or next husband came first. For those using charity events and fund-raising for social climbing purposes, the events they lent their names to came second, and so did making sure that funds were actually raised. These Ladies Who Lunch were in a league of their own—in league together and in love with their own press.

These PamperedPartyPrincesses were a very different breed than old money and even rough-around-the-edges nouvelle rich like DiamondDiva. Their spoiled and often shocking behavior left them looking much more like PettyPartyPrincesses—who had never left junior high school mentality behind or attended top charm/finishing schools like so many of them claimed to have done—than the envied and elitist PamperedPartyPrincesses they envisioned themselves to be and how they thought the world perceived them.

It was an eye-opening and at times jaw-dropping experience and no one ever fessed up to giving the leader of this pack of Petty-PartyPrincesses our telephone number. It was one hell of a ride while it lasted—trying to stay one step ahead of and out of the battling turf wars that took place between the alpha leaders of several PettyPrincess packs and their PettyPrincess ladies-in-waiting who were kept busy massaging the self-image of their leaders while planning and plotting their demise at the same time with their own coup d'état, while trying to make sure that the charity caught in the middle of all this inner circle fighting did not come out the loser. They, as were we, were dealing with egos that knew no bounds and who were dead set on marking their territory.

The bratty, prima donna and often vindictive antics of the PettyPartyPrincesses annoyed the heck out of Dee Dee and Daniela, who were more than ready and able to take them on in the name of good. They were more than a match for their tirades and tantrums. And Daniela could beat them at their own game (she easily out-dressed, out-classed and out-traveled them, having only traveled the world first class and stayed at the best-of-the-best resorts, as had Dee Dee and I) when they were being snotty and snarky around haute couture and the "shocking" fashion faux pas their competing PettyPartyPrincesses and their petulant and pouting ladies-in-waiting packs committed. The PettyPartyPrincesses wilted under Daniela's critical eye and sharp tongue when she turned it around and turned it on them after she felt they crossed the line of acceptable social behavior, and she wanted to put them in check. These PettyPartyPrincesses would never misplace their lipstick but they sure didn't have a problem mislaying their morals if they thought it would move them up one rung on the social ladder. Daniela was a master of giving a backhanded compliment. It's a shame that most of it went over their heads. But Dee Dee and others present, wealthy contributors who were there as true patrons to support the charity cause, often had difficulty hiding their smiles.

Dee Dee discovered a website devoted to tracking the Muffys and the Tiffanys in the world of socialites, their rankings, their clothes, their choices of dates, the events to which they lent their names and their SR Silver Spoon Awards. They had down pat the categories some of these Pampered and PettyPartyPrincesses aspired to:

SR Silver Spoon Awards Categories

- Socialite of the Year
- Socialite Event of the Year
- Socialite Career Highlight of the Year
- Socialite Couple of the Year
- Designer of the Year
- Socialite Campaign of the Year
- Breakthrough Socialite of the Year
- International Socialite Award
- Socialite Dress of the Year
- Socialite Press Clip of the Year
- Socialite Sibling Team of the Year

Dee Dee and Daniela had a few more categories they would have added after going several rounds with warring camps of Petty-PartyPrincesses and their ladies-in-waiting when there were two co-chairs hosting an event who tried nonstop to upstage one another with little regard for what they had signed on to do. Many of the nonprofit events the PettyPartyPrincesses undertook actually ended up running at a loss and costing the charities money instead of raising funds, which was not surprising because in many cases the events that PettyPartyPrincesses were undertaking or proposing were a means to get their names in the media, throw a gala party for their friends at no personal cost to them and increase their social status. All event elements were carefully contrived and orchestrated with military precision to further their personal social agenda and showcase them, not the charity.

Reigning **PamperedPettyPartyPrincess** Ladies-in-Waiting Rules

#1 It is *always* all about ME
#2 See rule #1 (all you really need to remember)

The nonprofit planners had our total respect for having to deal with the demanding and entitled attitudes of an event's ruling chairs and hosts when their charity aligned themselves with a PettyPartyPrincess type, having initially been taken in by dazzling monetary returns projections for a gala fund-raising endeavor headed by them but underwritten by the charity if their event did not raise money. They could have instead aligned their organization with a true patron of their cause (the other Ladies That Lunch Club/Respected Society Mavens) that had only their organization's well-being at heart and were prepared to put their time, energies and, in many cases, their own money into making their event a rewarding success.

One celebrity gala fund-raiser that ended up in the red, costing the charity thousands and thousands of dollars they did not have, only received $5,000 from the celebrity host. To add insult to injury, the celebrity host was perceived in the media as underwriting the entire cost for the event along with the PettyPartyPrincess who was anxious to link her name to theirs. The charity was just being used a PR tactic and society-positioning tool. Prices were set and tickets sold to only their Rolodex of personal friends and/or given to friends of the PettyPartyPrincess in lieu of their support for her—not for the nonprofit organization—before all the costs of the event were known and they came in much higher than the PettyPartyPrincess chair ever anticipated. That is, if she'd even given it that much thought. She'd done nothing to secure major corporate sponsors to help pay for the cost of the event so that the monies from all tickets sales plus silent auction items and donations went to the charity as profit. She did, however, spend money on a new designer gown, professional hair and makeup, new jewelry and her own personal photographer to make sure that she got all the pictures she wanted of herself with celebrities, other select top society folk and politicians gathered around her.

When the media queried the dollars raised, true figures could not be given because that would have been an admission that a great private party took place but unfortunately—too bad, so sad—no actual monies were raised, and in fact the charity went into the hole, and was left scrambling to find the funds to pay for their event. Sometimes charities do enter into this kind of arrangement knowing full well they are being used but hoping that having their organization shown as being in partnership with well-known names will help bring added exposure to their cause and make securing corporate sponsors the next go round easier.

For us, it was fascinating to see the social and political games being played for personal gain in another side of our industry and where being a master of discretion involved much more than we had encountered before. Sure, there were still the secret—or not so secret—affairs, misspent money, backstabbing, and unethical behavior we encountered on a daily basis but the level of cut-throatness of the PettyPartyPrincesses was something new added to the mix, as was the despair and unhappiness we saw when the veil got lifted at times and we were able to see what was driving these PettyPartyPrincesses.

We learned that all the money in the world doesn't buy you class and doesn't ensure happiness. Many of these women lived their lives on the superficial surface and radiated being miserable from deep inside. Many of their marriages had been fueled by their love of money, not the men in their lives. We witnessed mothers who had been groomed to marry money or marry into a higher social status doing the same with their daughters—and that was another purpose of getting involved in society gala fund-raising. One PettyPartyPrincess mom gushed at how her daughter just "loved" dating much older businessmen and she worked the seating chart like a mom on a marriage mission. Her daughter was 17. For many PettyPartyPrincesses, social climbing was their career and a way of furthering their husband's career. They had to look the part, play the part and produce the business and social connection results their spouses were looking for or there was hell to pay at home. After all, they could easily be replaced by a younger PettyPartyPrincess model.

Daniela witnessed one PettyPartyPrincess's meltdown at home when she discovered a miniscule pulled thread in her designer gown that she was going to wear that evening and dissolved into tears telling Daniela that "she just didn't understand how important being and looking perfect was and that her husband was going to be furious with her about the tiny—invisible to almost every naked eye—flaw in her dress." She, along with her gown, would be perceived as damaged goods. It was essential to her livelihood that she be considered a prize accessory on her husband's arm.

Daniela was able to share with her tricks from her past haute couture modeling days and restore the PettyPartyPrincess's spirits, all the while knowing inside that what had just taken place would not stop the PettyPartyPrincess from mocking someone else's misfortune that night should they be viewed as less than perfect in the eyes of her peers—but at least it was someone else and not her.

Behind their façade of flashy jewelry, fake smiles and air kisses (PettyPartyPrincesses know not to muss their dress, makeup or hair) and their seemingly narcissistic belief that they looked more fabulous than anyone else in the room, things were not always as they appear. There was a great deal of insecurity, along with insincerity, lurking there. And if the PettyPartyPrincesses sometimes wrapped themselves in protective layers of expensive fur coats bought by their "adoring" husbands, or so they said, it could be from trying to warm themselves from the frozen iciness some of their spouses displayed towards them when they were not on show. Working with them in their homes, you could often cut the tension between picture-perfect couples with a knife, and you found yourself wishing for something with which to ward off the chill. Their entitled arrogance, while very real, is also used as a self-defense mechanism.

A PettyPartyPrincess, Dee Dee, Daniela and I learned, is a type of woman that wants something at all cost, will do almost anything to get it, and never says thank you, but man, can the personal price be high. Wouldn't want to be one nor spend my life energies working with them to further their demanding diva goals. I'd rather work with DiamondDivas any day. While DiamondDiva may be a connoisseur (in her own mind) of expensive trinkets and toys and had tons of rough edges, she did have a truly expansive heart when it came to making sure that "her kids" were taken care of and thanked. She knew that they buttered her bread, provided her with oceans of champagne and she gave back, but not only to them. She was also a big patron supporter, with no strings attached, to charities and causes she believed in.

Under the umbrella of event planning there are three very distinct areas and each is suited to a very specific personality type. One category is made up of corporate and business social event planners, another of personal party planners (wedding planners and all the festivities related to that, family or society celebrations like sweet 16s and bar and bat mitzvahs) and the third of nonprofit association planners who work in-house with the charity.

Corporate and business social event planners are skilled in event psychology, which requires the ability to strategically develop events that deliberately create and/or target specific responses and motivate their client's attendees by tapping into people's personal and professional dreams to bring their clients the return on their event investment (time, money and energy) they desire. There is a world of difference between "party planning" (weddings, birthday parties and other personal celebrations) and professional corporate and social results-driven "event planning," which can still include seemingly personal celebrations—such as an awards ceremony or personal anniversary—but they come wrapped with a business agenda as does any gala fund-raiser to which a company lends their name and company image. Corporate and business social event planners are used to working with big budgets and dealing with one key decision-maker.

Party planners and wedding planners are working in an event planning arena that can require a lot of hand-holding and dealing with a multitude of emotions—not evoking them in the manner a corporate and business social event planner does, but rather calming them and the frayed nerves of multiple self-deemed de-cision-makers (think of a wedding: the bride, groom, mother of the bride, father of the bride, mother of the groom, father of the groom, maids of honor, best men, relatives on both sides, and well-meaning friends all clamor to be heard). Most corporate and social business event planners run for the hills when their family, friends or clients ask them to take on a personal party event. They don't have the patience for hand-holding. That's not what makes them tick. Instead, it's meeting corporate business challenges cre-ativity through custom events that fulfills them. They don't want to hear 27 different options on which shade of buttercup yellow is the perfect shade. They want to only hear their own creative voice, knowing that what they choose will be the right one. They are not adept at handling what in their minds is time-wasting and money-wasting frou frou. They are results driven and business minded, while still wanting to produce meaningful, memorable, magical events but not wanting to deal with emotional decision-making and a limited budget. Corporate and business social event planners *can* work with limited funds but prefer not to deal with bridezillas whose demands far exceed money supply.

Nonprofit event planners deserve a medal. Their job requires them to handle elements of both and struggle to obtain sponsorship dollars and support when thousands of other charities are doing the same thing. Nonprofit planners, unlike professional corporate and business social event planners and party planners, don't have an experienced team of staff and suppliers to help them pull off an event. And there's no money to hire one. They are working with volunteers who may know absolutely nothing about timing, logistics and successful event execution and they don't know what they don't know. Then again, sometimes neither does the in-house nonprofit planner who may have just been thrust into that role. And at some events Dee Dee, Daniela and I witnessed, we saw volunteers that did not even honor their commitment to show up and fulfill their duties. At one event fewer than half the volunteers showed up to set up and run the nonprofit's event. Remember, just like the PamperedPettyPartyPrincesses, volunteers can come with their own set of agendas, including meeting Mr. Right or gaining entrance into society circles. Not all of them are there because they are passionate about the cause.

Jumping in and working with them was a learning experience on both sides. After seeing the disastrous results of gala fund-raiser event left in PettyPartyPrincess hands and experiencing the chaos and confusion, we knew that the best way we could support charities was to contribute in other ways that would be of more value to us and to the charities and that wouldn't leave Dee Dee, Daniela and me banging our heads on the table as we saw money walk out the door time and time again. We couldn't risk our company name being tied to an event with less than stellar results, especially since we would have only handled a part of it and probably would have been called in only a day, a week or just several weeks before the event to try and save it from cancellation disaster and hefty cancellation charges. The only way we could take on another nonprofit event was if we brought in a corporate sponsor willing to underwrite the entire event—as a marketing tool for them around brand awareness of their company, to access to their target audience, to introduce a new product, as a public relations maneuver, or so that they're viewed as a company who gives back—and do it in the polished and professional manner of how their corporate events are run. We kept saying that someone needs to write a book—and someone did write an entire best-selling series after experiencing what we did and seeing the same need—and tell PettyPartyPrincesses how to properly hold such a function. But unless it was wrapped in a fashion magazine, it was doubtful they'd ever read it.

"You just don't understand," said one Princess in a self-important tone. "It's attitude." It was attitude, all right, but not the kind she was talking about. "ChattyCattyCathy" went on to say that of course people (her people) would adhere to the code of high society etiquette, inferring that Dee Dee, Daniela and I knew nothing about such behavior, and that if their invitation reads from 6 to 10 they will leave promptly at 10 and the ones coming from 9 to 12 will not arrive early. Experience tells us that, high society or not, they were setting themselves up for major problems and risking having their gala fund-raising event closed down with television cameras rolling. When you take the gala opening of a new cutting-edge entertainment complex and invite families—not just couples—to attend and in the hopes of having maximum attendance set it up as a two-tier event with time overlap and no means of regulating who extended or came early, and combine that with free food, free drinks, top entertainment, high-energy bands, high-tech special effect indoor laser shows and a fireworks finale, no one's leaving until the very end.

This is very different from doing a day event followed by an evening event with the venue closing down at the end, the facilities being refreshed and then reopening. There you have some semblance of controlling guest count numbers and adhering to fire marshal regulations. And you should have heard the gasps when we told them that porta potties—yes, we found luxury ones—would have to be set up in an area out of sight in order to get the go-ahead for the doors to be open based on the invited numbers.

Thankfully we were just sharing our expertise, not taking on or tackling this fund-raising event, and came in at the beginning to give them a heads up. In support of the charity, we did purchase tickets to the gala event and exactly as predicted "attitude" meant zip when it came to parents leaving at their appointed time when they had their children begging to stay and knew there was no way someone could tell if they were on the early or late invitee list. As all of us left at the "correct" time, we encountered Chatty CattyCathy out front begging the fire department—in not so nice tones—not to close their event down and not to walk through the building (which of course they did). The volunteer minions were trying to calm down a huge line of parents and their very unhappy children waiting to get into the venue and were racing to and fro trying to appease them by bringing out food and soft drinks. The press on hand were getting wonderful candid shots of a foot-stomping PettyPartyPrincess losing total control of herself and her event as the men in uniform marched through the building and worked to bring numbers down before shutting down the gala. A much different grand finale than had been planned.

A knowing attitude is very different than knowing attitudes—which we did. Dee Dee and Daniela made sure to stop by and pay their respects just when ChattyCattyCathy was turning different shades of red, which really did not go with her dress, as Daniela deliberately stage-whispered just a teeny tiny bit cattily to Dee Dee.

The event that was triggered by a frantic telephone call was one where major celebrities were attending and tickets had been sold out, but not one bit of work had been done on the actual event because none of the ladies-in-waiting had been able to make the meetings or time for this event and they were now in the middle of prime personal entertaining season and family getaways to second and third homes. Even though the event had been planned for months, the two PettyPartyPrincess co-chairs were so at each other's throats and busy sabotaging one another—and trying to best each other in who could pull in the highest social ranking celebrities and guests—that actual event operations had gone unnoticed and undone until two weeks before the event was to take place. Now they were in full panic mode and rightly so.

We took a look at the venue and what had to be done. It's one thing to pull off an event for 2,000 in under six weeks with professional help and a budget to pay for what needed to be done, but it's an entirely different matter to try and take something high profile on and do it with no dollars, no expert supplier and no program director help. Because of the nature of the event—a celebration of someone's lifetime of achievements—we jumped in and enlisted an army of event planning industry friends to save this event for the award recipient (who was greatly beloved by the world and had no clue what was going on or in this case not going on). We certainly didn't do it to save the PettyPartyPrincesses' faces or fates should the press who were coming out in droves catch wind of what had been left undone. While the two PettyPartyPrincesses battled it out for control as to who would sit next to the top guest of honor, etc., everyone worked around the clock for two weeks straight to pull this off. It was touch and go right down to the wire,

with everyone doing it on their own end as a labor of love or re-spect for the guest's talents and contributions to the world.

We met attitude again in suggesting that one of the PettyParty-Princess chairs not try and arrive at the event with the celebrated guest but rather be on hand to welcome her guests and entertain the press while they were waiting, but nothing would deter her from making a grand entrance with the VIP. It would be a great photo op and all that, stepping out of the limo with them clearly showing that they were BFFs. She was hell-bent on stealing the limelight and following PettyPartyPrincess rule #1—It is *always* all about ME—to the max. For her, that night was about showing the guest, the press and the public at large that she, not her co-chair, was the reigning PettyPartyPrincess.

Sigh ... we tried to tell her. The newspapers the next day and television entertainment news clips showed Dee Dee proudly welcoming the guest as they stepped out of the limousine and the press surrounding them with flashbulbs going off and everyone asking for sound bites. And when the wannabe QueenPettyPar-tyPrincess dramatically stepped out of the limousine to grace everyone with her presence not a soul was left around, as ev-eryone had followed the star of the evening in with her co-chair, linking arms with them and appearing not to ever consider letting go. The co-chair had also managed to be the center of attention, entertaining the press while they waited for the limousine to ar-rive. And it would have been her, not Dee Dee, who actually would have been the one to greet the guest had she not been pulled away to be interviewed by a news station live. Then again, it would have been the wannabe QueenPettyPartyPrincess doing the grand deed—being part of the live television interview—if she had been ready when the limousine and VIP guests arrived to pick her up. They had set off without her knowing how im-portant timing was, but returned to pick her up when she threw an incredible tantrum when she discovered they were no longer waiting. She was adamant that she arrive in the limo with the celebrity guest. Have to admit that after all we had been put through, seeing wannabe QueenPettyPartyPrincess's face when she stepped out of the limousine, and there was no one, to pose for was priceless.

You would have thought we'd learned our lesson by now, but nope. It's hard for those in the industry who take event orchestration very seriously not to step in and try and do something if they see an event about to go off track. We still did what we could when we could but at a distance.

We jumped in the day before an event to try and track down over 1,000 martini glasses for a fund-raising event that advertised a martini bar. No one had remembered to check if the venue they were holding the event at actually had them on hand. Nope. Had to be rented at a cost in the thousands and paid for by the non-profit organization.

Another time we found a restaurant willing to lend a gala event bottled water when the donated shipment got tied up in customs and would not make it on time and of course it was a brand not easily found. This was high-society palates, after all, that we were saving from being parched and ordinary tap water would not do, and if water was purchased it would come off of the charity's bottom line.

We even ended up doing bussing and dish-washing duty at one fund-raising event that featured gourmet food tasting—one that we were paid guests at—when it turned out that volunteers did not show and it appeared the expected number of guests was more than the restaurants had dishes, glasses and cutlery for. With each sampling guests were laying down their dirty plates and heading off in search of fresh ones. Matters were made worse when one restaurant decided to use the wine glasses on hand for their desserts, and so there we were dealing with patrons' parched throats again. The dishwasher in the venue was slow; no one had tested or timed it and they had not hired staff to bus, load, unload or replace, counting on volunteers to take on that duty. No wonder the volunteers didn't show when they were given their assignments.

And major upsets occurred in the cloakroom when the volunteers that had checked in the coats checked out and left.

We should have done the same when we arrived and saw the stage for the fashion show being carried out because it didn't fit and we watched bottles of champagne disappearing upstairs with the models. The writing was on the wall right there, but we didn't get out while the getting was good. Dee Dee said she was mortified when one of our top clients saw her carrying a stack of dirty dishes to the kitchen, praying that they did not think this was an event that she was responsible for. That was a wake-up call to the damage we could easily do to our reputation if we did not step away from run-and-rescue missions.

And we tried to tell them that one bathroom serving hundreds of guests in a venue that was about to be torn down was not a good idea. And you can imagine the outcome. It wasn't pretty nor pleasant and guests left early because within an hour they could no longer use the facilities. Luckily for the PettyPartyPrincesses the fire marshal had not caught wind of what they were doing.

The final breaking point when we made good our escape from the Ladies Who Lunch speed dial was at one fund-raising gala where no audiovisual rehearsals were done, even though we had stressed over and over how necessary this was. When the moment came to see the show, with over a thousand people sitting in the ballroom, the equipment turned out not to be working. That was before the fire alarm and sprinkler system went off after a fire broke out in the back corridors from the device used to set off the indoor pyro centerpieces at each table by someone who had no experience. As guests hastily departed, they did stop long enough to take home—or divide up—the centerpieces, which were only borrowed not bought, and the nonprofit organization ended up having to pay for them as well.

We decided we were much safer and could contribute in a way that would be better for all involved by working with our corporate clients when they decided to sponsor a gala fund-raiser to help them create standout events that produced desired results for all involved as well as protecting their interests, the nonprofit organization's and our own from those with a social agenda and hopefully bring nonprofit event planners a bit of a break from working nonstop with the PettyPartyPrincesses and their ladies-in-waiting.

The holiday tea we did with one corporate client was a tremendous financial success. The ballroom was filled with designer and celebrity decorated Christmas trees—you could smell the scent of pine from the lobby—that were to be auctioned off and delivered to the winning home (or hospital, nursing home, etc. of their choice). The event was heartwarming from beginning till end and put everyone in a festive mood. The silent auction offered items perfect for holiday gifts. Everyone came out a winner. It wasn't a case of building an event that was all about ME, the chair, but crafting one that would be of value to all involved.

One corporate sponsored nonprofit event that always warmed our hearts was the travel company that flew terminally ill children to the North Pole every year on a flight to nowhere. Santa and his helpers would emerge from the cockpit and distribute gifts to the children and give their family members a lifelong lasting memory. Doesn't get much better than seeing children's faces filled with happiness and wonder after returning home from the North Pole.

Yup, give us our DiamondDiva's attitude of caring instead of catering to a DemandingDiva's any day. Dee Dee, Daniela and I all agreed that doing what we do and how we do it is a fit for who we are and what we love to do, and that our Ladies That Lunch club (with only PettyPartyPrincesses and their ladies-in-waiting as members, who operate very differently from the Ladies That Lunch club/Respected Society Mavens members) experiences left us the wiser as to what is truly important in life. We discovered that being masters of discretion had served us, and those we worked with and for, well.

SOCIAL AGENDAS: Q&A

Corporate Events vs. Nonprofit Events

Q: What is a one of the main differences between working on a corporate event and on a nonprofit event?

A: With corporate events you have an assigned budget and multiple event objectives to be met and you are working with an executive team committed to reaching those goals. With a nonprofit event you have the added challenge of raising, or waiting, for sponsorship dollars to be raised and you are often working with committee chairs and volunteers who do not have an event planning background and do not necessarily understand all the timing and logistical requirements of some of their demands. They are also giving their time, and their personal and professional responsibilities can often take priority over volunteer time commitments.

Assignment

Discuss how event planning companies can work effectively with nonprofit committees and stay in control of their time and not be fielding numerous calls coming in. (Answer: one way is by appointing one specific person to be the main contact person as opposed to having all the committee members have access to calls.)

Cause Marketing

Q: Why would corporations want to partner with nonprofit organizations and run their own event with them?

A: Cause marketing is very important today. It gives a corporation a chance to showcase their company and the good work that they are doing. It brings brand awareness and good PR and introduces their company to a very targeted market audience.

It is important to align the corporation, the cause and the event. For example, holding a charity golf tournament and having strippers doing lap dances and serving drinks on the course would not be appropriate nor play out well in the press. There needs to be a fit. For example, one financial district does a very successful race through the downtown streets with the runners dressed in business suits and carrying attaché cases. They make it fun and have created a way to get more press coverage than had runners worn traditional workout clothes.

Assignment

Discuss some examples of corporate fund-raising events and whether or not they were a good fit.

Nonprofit Event Challenges

Q: What is one of the most difficult aspects of doing a nonprofit event?

A: Making sure that there is sufficient time to secure sponsorship dollars. It takes time to research and contact the right corporate sponsors and get them to a yes, as well as to get dollars in from charity supporters. An event can run at a loss if there is not sufficient time to turn everything around. You need more than six months of planning time. With a corporate event you can turn it around in a matter of days or weeks if the dollars are there to make it happen.

Assignment

Choose a random charity and think about which corporate sponsors would be a fit—where there would be a mutual benefit and why.

Nonprofit Event Essentials

Q: What essential item should be costed in, as it will help the event be a success and pave the way for additional corporate involvement the next year?

A: Budget for experienced event planning staff as opposed to relying on volunteers to try and save dollars. If the event execution is not seamless, it will be difficult to attract the potential and existing corporate sponsors who may be attending to participate the following year.

Assignment

Where could volunteers be most effectively used during an event and what areas should be managed by event planning experts for best results? (Answer: securing and manning silent auction goods is one area at which volunteers excel.)

Managing Chairs and Their Committee Members

Q: How can you avoid having a clash of the egos between chair person heads?

A: Give each a specific area or areas of responsibility. They can compete to bring their best to their assigned areas as opposed

to competing among themselves on whose direction to follow if
they are both overseeing the same area.

Assignment

What would be some of the event element areas that the event
chairs could be actively involved in that would not cause upset
but allow them to shine. (Answer: some areas would include
preparing the guest list, selling tickets, managing RSVPs and
allocating the table seating.)

Non-financial Profits

Q: Is it ever okay for a charity event to run at a loss?

A: Yes. Sometimes cause awareness is the main objective, as
may be good media exposure that will help to pave the way for
sponsorship dollars for a major upcoming event.

Assignment

Discuss various types of charity events that receive excellent
media coverage year after year and why that may be. (Answer:
one would be tied to celebrity event endorsement.)

Nonprofit Concerns for Event Planners

Q: When taking on a charity event, what do event planning companies need to be aware of?

A: They will be judged on the event execution. And they need
to realize that some of their corporate clients could be there
as guests, and it will reflect back on the planning company
should an event not come across as polished and professional

because volunteers and not expert event planning staff were being used to save dollars.

Assignment

Discuss other ways that event planning companies can take part in charity events and still maintain complete event orchestration control. (Answer: one way is by proposing that a corporate client create and underwrite a charity event in full and work closely with the charity to make sure that both sets of event objectives are met.)

Aligning Client and Cause

Q: What do corporate sponsors look for when selecting a charity?

A: Corporate sponsors want to work with charities that are professional, appeal to their target market audience, attract maximum attendance and media exposure and whose cause is in alignment with their corporate culture.

Assignment

Discuss ways that a charity organization can effectively market their event to potential corporate sponsors. (Answer: one way is to invite corporate decision-makers as their guests to this year's event so that they can see firsthand how their event is run.)

Volunteering

Q: Can professional event planning companies and event planners benefit from volunteering their time and their talents in a controlled manner?

A: For event planners starting out and looking to gain experience with different styles of events, nonprofit gala events can be an excellent place to learn what not to do and what to do. One event planning company used volunteering at nonprofit events as a marketing tool to grow their client base. They deliberately sought out high-profile events chaired by PartyPrincesses because of their social standing, the circles they moved in and the business contacts they could—and did—introduce them to.

Assignment

List the various ways event planners can work with nonprofit organizations to the mutual benefit of both companies.

CHAPTER

12 ROCKING THE CASBAH

Em has another encounter with DiamondDiva but this time around she is going in knowing exactly what to expect and how to handle her client demands in a way that causes her no stress and protects her client, her company and her own composure.

DECEMBER 13

What a week. Just back from a whirlwind site inspection with DiamondDiva and Wills, covering one end of Morocco to the other by private—white, of course—stretch limousine through the Atlas Mountains. Casablanca, Marrakech, Fez, Rabat and Meknes were just a few of our stops. DiamondDiva was in her element. Champagne was within arm's reach for the duration of the trip but was carefully monitored, and we ensured there were numerous stops so that she was not just sitting in the limo and drinking for extended periods of time. Bright, shiny, expensive objects were still very effective in distracting DiamondDiva from drinking. They are her true passion.

And we fed her love of adventure. Staying in palaces. Bargaining for jewelry in the medina and souks. Rescuing a blonde-haired and blue-eyed young maiden who begged us for help, as she came upon us and our guide in the maze. DiamondDiva being rescued in return from the snake charmers in Djemaa el-Fna Square in Marrakech. DiamondDiva ordering bastila (pronounced *basteela* and translated means pigeon pie) for all of us to dine upon, and electing to sleep in the limo overnight as opposed to any of the hotels we saw in one area. Shudder. Taking part in a traditional hand washing ceremony, where rosewater is poured from a silver urn, before being served a typical Moroccan dinner of salads, couscous, tajine, lamb and other local specialties in a private tent in the middle of the desert and being entertained by folkloric dances, while sitting on thick Moroccan carpets with traditional low tables. Watching an exhibit of Arabian horses ridden by acrobats and cavaliers demonstrating traditional forms of old military combat under a desert sky filled with stars with a flaming grand finale. Just another typical week at the office, but with a much longer commute.

Can't believe a year has already gone by and it's starting to become a tradition that I spend part of my December with DiamondDiva, but this trip was so much better because we now had a handle on our client and an understanding of her—and her participants'—needs. That is the beauty of repeat business, which often leads to referral business: you get to know how to choose exactly the right event elements that will be a fit for your client.

I hadn't been back in Northern Africa since I had traveled there on a site inspection alone when I first started out in the business. That had been a learning adventure. And it stirred up a lot of old memories. I had placed my self in unsafe situations a couple of times by being too trusting and forgiving too easily. If the general manager of one of the hotels had not turned on the radio in his car when he did while were were supposedly on our way to dinner and heard the news that made it imperative to get immediately back to his hotel, I don't know what would have happened back then up on that lonely mountaintop when he kept saying, "Nice girls say no but they really mean yes"—but that's a story to be shared someday at a later time.

Right now it's time to decompress DiamondDiva, catch up with loved ones and make my way slowly into the office. Note to self: I have got to learn to start requesting advance copies of menus when traveling with DiamondDiva. Thank goodness she missed seeing camel meat on the menu.

Next week I am heading back out again, this time to the South Pacific on a luxury yacht cruise that we have taken over exclusively for our client and his guests. Only Daniela will be staying behind. An incredible week is planned, complete with dinner served by tuxedoed waiters in the ocean. Will be well worth the longer commute to get to our floating office. . . .

Rocking the Casbah: Assignment

Design an overview of a seven-day program in Morocco that would hold appeal to DiamondDiva and list the important event elements that would need to be included in her program. Make notes on what staff would need to be aware of (past learning lessons from other chapters that would apply to any DiamondDiva event, e.g., make sure that staff do not dress in a manner that outshines DiamondDiva, arrange security for purse full of gems).

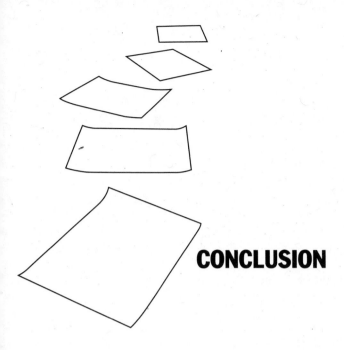

CONCLUSION

The past 12 chapters have introduced various real-life situations that show the value of having company policies, procedures and protocol in place, and illustrate that having a thorough understanding of what can be done—or should not be done—in emergency situations will serve to protect all involved. For example, if Em had listened to DiamondDiva's pleas not to let the crew see her when she was ill from too much drinking and not summoned medical personnel and if Diamond Diva had ended up having alcohol poisoning, or slipped and fell getting in and out of the shower, or choked if left on her own while still incapacitated, a lawsuit could have been the end result. The appropriate course of action was to summon professional help and to write up a report that would serve as legal backup.

There are times when you will be able to clearly assess the situation unfolding before you and follow the required course of action established by the agency and company lawyers, and there will be other times when you will not have a moment to think, such as when MrArrogance attempted to push his superior through a plate glass window. If emergency policies, procedures and protocol has not been established and discussed in advance around what needs to be done and where and why security had to be brought in to handle the situation, precious moments would have been lost and the situation could have escalated out of control in front of the guests. Had staff instinctively acted to physically stop the fight, they would have found themselves in the middle of it instead of moving into programmed crisis management control.

Sending staff out unprepared or allowing yourself to go out unprepared as to required company codes of conduct is irresponsible and can have serious legal, personal and professional repercussions. You can plan an event, you can anticipate all that can go right and wrong, and you can have a backup plan, but if you neglect to establish company policies, procedures and protocol and outline expected codes of conduct and crisis management courses of actions, then you have missed an essential step in successful event execution and in running a successful business that has the best interests of their employees, their suppliers, their clients and their guests.

You can never know what will happen when you combine people, personalities and a partying environment—and that combination is not limited to being on-site during an event. One event planning company, attending supplier functions at a trade show, took the right step in hiring a limousine to take them from party to party but they forgot they were still attending business functions *and* that they were not just partying with their peers but corporate clients as well. Their behavior, as company representatives, was so obnoxious that clients attending the event wanted to know which event planning company they worked with so that they could avoid doing business with them. That was a very costly event for the event planning company to find their employees displaying a total lack of professionalism. Establishing personal as well as company policies, procedures and protocol will elevate your company's commitment to professionalism and should be regarded as an essential event element.